Also in The Crafts Series from Little, Brown —
Gerald Clow, General Editor:

BLACK AND WHITE PHOTOGRAPHY
HENRY HORENSTEIN

LEATHERWORK
BENJAMIN MALESON

POTTERY
CORA PUCCI

CROCHET
MARY TIBBALS VENTRE

FORTHCOMING:
STAINED GLASS
BARBARA FRAZIER and GERRY CLOW

WEAVING
ELFLEDA RUSSELL

WOODWORK

WOODWORK

A Basic Manual

RAPHAEL TELLER

LITTLE, BROWN AND COMPANY—BOSTON—TORONTO

First Edition

T10/74

The author is extremely grateful to the following manufacturers for their permission to reprint the photographs on the pages indicated below:

Middlesex Welding Supply Company (lower right, 18)

Rockwell International (right-hand photograph, 14; 15; lower right photograph, 17; top left photograph, 18; 20; 22; top left and right-hand photographs, 23; left-hand photograph, 24; lower right photograph, 25; 26)

Sand-Rite Manufacturing Company (lower left, 23)

The Stanley Works (12; three left-hand photographs, 14; 16; top right photograph, 17; top right and lower left photographs, 18; left-hand and top right photographs, 19; left-hand and top right photographs, 21; right-hand photographs, 24; top right photograph, 25; left-hand photograph, 27; 28; left-hand photograph, 29)

Woodcraft Supply Corporation (10; 13; left-hand photograph, 17; lower right photograph, 19; lower left photograph, 21; left-hand photograph, 25; right-hand photographs, 27; right-hand photograph, 29)

The drawings and photographs in this book are by the author.

Published simultaneously in Canada by Little, Brown & Company (Canada) Limited

LIBRARY OF CONGRESS CATALOGING IN PUBLICATION DATA
Teller, Raphael.   Woodwork.   (The Crafts series)
1. Woodwork — Amateurs' manuals.   I. Title.
TT185.T35   684'.08   74-8319   ISBN 0-316-83655-9   ISBN 0-316-83656-7 (pbk.)
Printed in The United States of America

*Dedicated
to all Woodworkers*

Acknowledgments

Gerald Clow, general counsel
Linda Teller, typing
Richard McDonough and Leslie Arnold, editing at Little, Brown
R. W. Shattuck & Company Hardware, Arlington, Massachusetts
The many others who helped along the way.

Contents

The Little, Brown Crafts Series is designed and published for the express purpose of giving the beginner—usually a person trained to use his head, not his hands—an idea of the basic techniques involved in a craft, as well as an understanding of the inner essence of that medium. Authors were sought who do not necessarily have a "name" but who thoroughly enjoy sharing their craft, and all their sensitivities to its unique nature, with the beginner. Their knowledge of their craft is vital, although it was realized from the start that one person can never teach all the techniques available.

The series helps the beginner gain a sense of the spirit of the craft he chooses to explore, and gives him enough basic instruction to get him started. Emphasis is laid on creativity, as crafts today are freed from having to be functional; on process, rather than product, for in the making is the finding; and on human help, as well as technical help, as so many prior teaching tools have said only "how" and not "why." Finally, the authors have closed their books with as much information on "next steps" as they could lay their hands on, so that the beginner can continue to learn about the craft he or she has begun.

Gerald Clow

Introduction

What Wood Means to Me

The care that goes into thoughtfully planned and well-made woodwork shows in the finished pieces. In this way your attitude as a woodworker as much as your creations is handed down to your grandchildren. Who knows, the jury of time could render your work antique. Respect that a tree takes years and years to grow and build in such a way that what you make will last. Yes, you could have used wax, clay, metals, plastics or cardboard or a combination of them. Each medium has its own peculiarities. But you chose wood, the imperfect organic cellular construction material. I got hung up on wood early in life and still enjoy discovering its subtleties. It's an anthropomorphic material. When you go against the grain, it breaks up. When you don't allow for movement or the drying is uneven, it can crack or check. When you apply a good finish and rub it down well, the job looks it and you feel it. This quest for perfection and immortality brings to mind a little episode.

Twelve quarters back I helped deliver a crib I made up for a client. It was planned and made in one piece, permanently joined. "And I want to pass it down to the grandchildren," he had said. John arrived early one snowy evening, eager to load the crib aboard his compact station wagon. As we couldn't fit the crib inside, we loaded it aloft, giving the wagon a noble crown. Although we cleared the front door at John's all right, the top of the crib jammed into the ceiling about halfway up the first flight of stairs at the turn, and brought out the landlord on the first floor to find out what was going on. We decided to try the fire escape.

Mary lowered her new clothesline, which we hitched to the crib. Then we went up three stories to the top platform of the fire escape, to haul. We'd heave and gain a few feet, then anchor the clothesline on the top rail and rest momentarily. At about the second story, wind up and snow gusting, the crib jammed in a nearby tree. We freed it with padded ski poles. Finally we got the crib inside, where we took a premature victory break to get warmed up.

On the last stretch, the crib jammed in the hall at the turn into the selected bedroom. The outraged kid was bawling her head off on the floor, kicking her feet wildly in the air as the clock struck twelve. After removing several door casings to no profit, John decided to slot the hall wall plaster with an old chisel to allow clearance. Finally we made it, and the kid fell asleep quickly in her new quarters, making it all seem worthwhile. John became all smiles, quite pleased with his evening's accomplishment. If you had stuck him with a pin, which I would have if I'd had one, he would have popped.

I had a quick cup of coffee and drove home in the continuing snowstorm. I went inside and sat down in the living room with the lights off for an hour or so wondering whether the preceding four hours had happened or were dreamed. In other words, try to make it "knock-downable" so that delivery is as uncomplicated as possible.

And at any rate, welcome to woodwork. I'm offering a basic approach in this book for the interested and motivated person who wants to work with wood as an amateur or as a professional. I'll be writing from my own experience. I'll begin with my estimate of the complement of tools and equipment needed, their maintenance, safety considerations, and woodworking techniques. The book will then proceed by categories with my photographs and illustrations—shelves, tables, chairs, beds and sofas, cabinetry, and small outbuildings; design considerations for further study, and suggestions concerning the small business operation. I believe in learning by doing, and this book is a guide along the way.

You will find fundamentals to work with here and I feel they are tried and true. You will not be overburdened with meticulous instruction and many demands. I try to keep it simple yet to the point. If the book were three times as long it probably could not cover all the situations that come up, and as you work you'll develop the processes and techniques best for you. Wood may not be as moldable as clay and definitely can be said to require certain standard approaches. Nonetheless, there are about twenty ways to do a given operation or project that will work. Or one way with twenty variations. Pick your own way as you find what's best for you and be happy.

Tools and Equipment

Buy the best you can afford. You can't expect good work without good tools. The best are none too good and the worst are far too bad. You needn't buy all the tools at once and they needn't be new. The old wood planes and chisels can be inexpensive (bought second-hand or at auction) and the tool steel can be better than the new ones. So check the newspaper for woodwork auctions. You can improvise with a few hand tools at first; the most important ones are starred below. You can buy your wood already dressed (smooth) and ready to go. As the projects get larger and you get fussier, power tool performance becomes important. Locally, see your best quality hardware store and lumberyard. Check your telephone Yellow Pages for woodwork suppliers. Also I recommend the following mail-order houses from experience; be sure to send for the catalogs, where you'll find additional tools.

Brookstone Company
14 Brookstone Building
Peterborough, New Hampshire 03458

Silvo Hardware
107–109 Walnut Street
Philadelphia, Pennsylvania 19106

Woodcraft Supply Corp.
313 Montvale Avenue
Woburn, Massachusetts 01801

The following list can serve as a guide to equip your shop. The asterisked items are what you need initially; an estimate for these new tools in 1974 was approximately $75.

• *Abrasives,* 60X, 80X, 100X, 120X, 150X, 220X aluminum oxide. 400X, 600X silicon carbide. Three standard 9 x 11 sheets each to start with.
• *Bench,* genuine woodworking, hardwood, bench stops, face and end vise. You can build your own, but I suggest buying one. At least have a sturdy wood top worktable to clamp stock to.

Danish workbench with tool tray, shoulder vise, end vise and two sets of bench stops

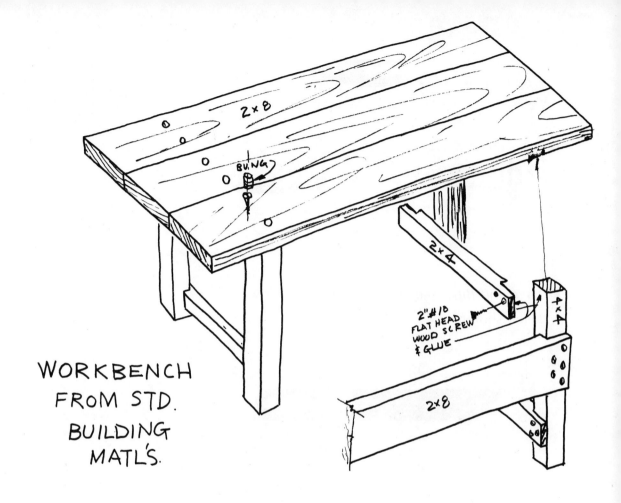

2 x 8

BUNG

2 x 4

2" #10
FLAT HEAD
WOOD SCREW
& GLUE

4 x 4

2 x 8

WORKBENCH
FROM STD.
BUILDING
MATL'S.

STOCK LIST FORM

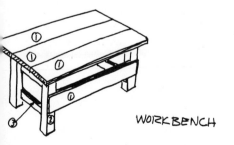

WORKBENCH

PART#	THICKNESS		WIDTH		QUANTITY	/	LENGTH IN INCHES, VARIABLE TO PERSONAL REQUIREMENTS
①	2	×	8	×	5	/	72
②	4	×	4	×	4	/	28
③	2	×	4	×	4	/	24

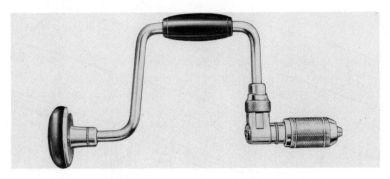

Yankee brace

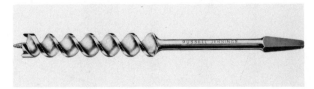

Auger bit for brace

- *Brace and Bits.* See electric drill sizes below.
- *Bevel,* sliding.

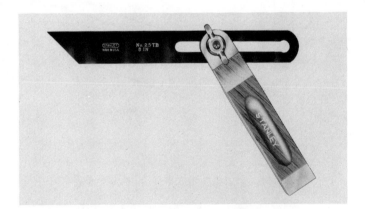

Sliding T-bevel

- **Broom.*
- **Box or chest* for tools.
- **Brushes,* bristle 2½, 3 inches; *bench brush, dust-pan type.

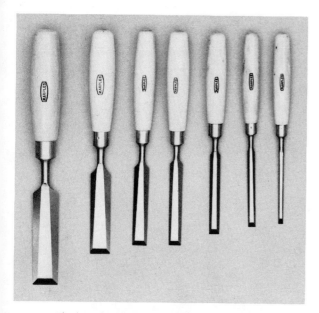

Flat bench chisels, beveled edges good for
dovetailing

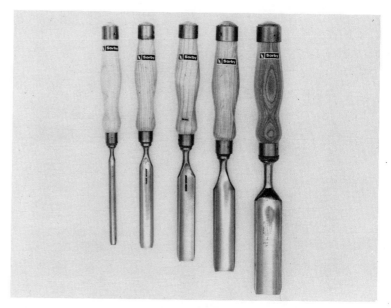

Curved chisel gouge

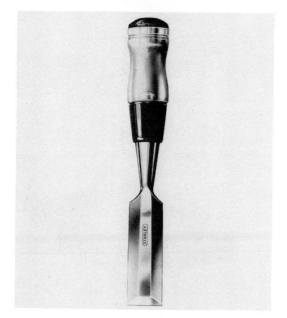

Butt chisel

• *Chisels,* flat bench type, *¼-, ½-, *¾-, 1-inch. 8-
gouge (curved chisel) 7, 16, 25 m/m.

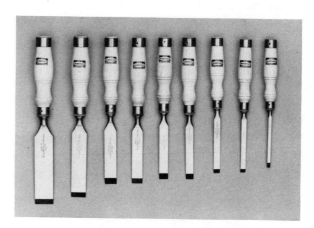

Heavy-duty flat chisels, square edges good for mortising

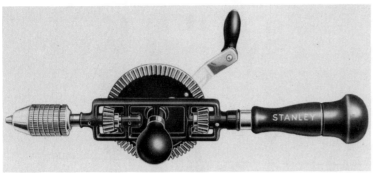
Hand drill, eggbeater type

Push drill, assorted drill bits in handle

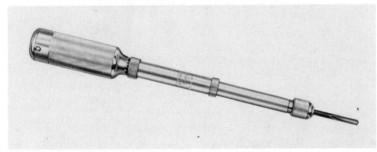

• *Clamps,* bar or pipe. Four 4-foot, four 3-foot. Needed for gluing up work. Length depends on size of piece. Four hand screws, 10–14-inch jaw length. Needed for gluing up and in lieu of vise and bench stops. Need at least two.

• *Drills,* eggbeater type, push type.

• *Drill press* up to 2,800 rpm with mortise attachment, $5/16$ hollow chisel bit, brad point bits.

Brad point bit, single spur

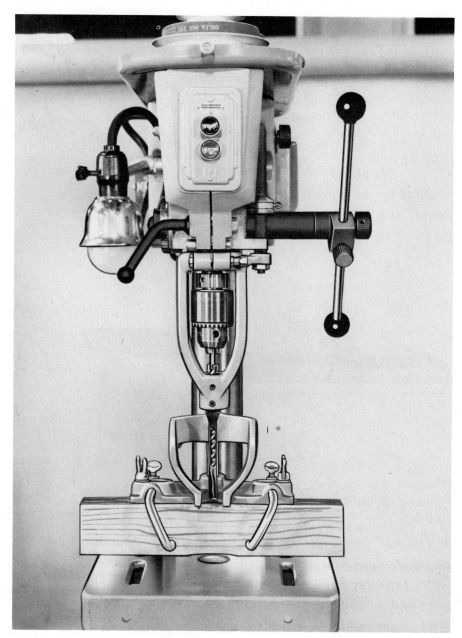

Mortise attachment for drill press

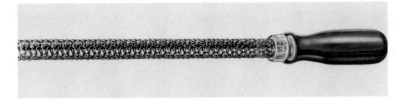

Surform round file

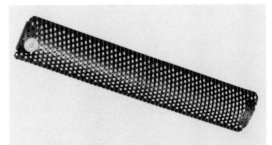

• *Files*. Bit file. 12-inch mill single cut. Flat 12-inch Multikut. 7-inch Slim Taper. Surform half round and round. File card to clean files.

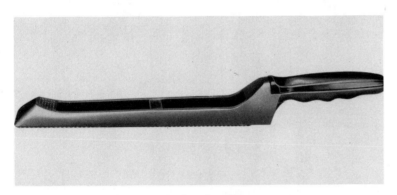

Surform handle

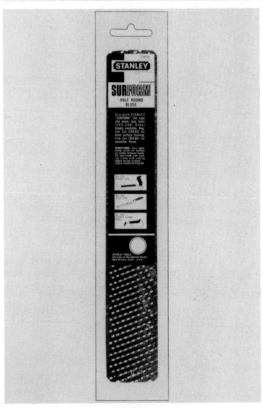

Surform half-round blade, to use with Surform file

• *Fire extinguisher*, 8-pound Tri-class works all kinds of fires.

• **Finishes*. Linseed oil, boiled or refined. *Paraffin oil, pure (Mobil Oil Prorex 905). *Rags, cheesecloth. Stain, powder, dark walnut and honey maple. Turpentine, steam-distilled. *Urethane, clear gloss.

• **First aid:* adhesive tape, bandages, gauze, Merthiolate.

Marking gauge

- *Gauge*, marking.
- *Glasses*, regular or goggles.
- **Glue*, white or yellow liquid. Weldwood powder.
- *Grinder*, bench. Fine, coarse aluminum oxide wheel, 6-inch-diameter minimum. Silicon carbide dressing stick to keep wheel trued up.

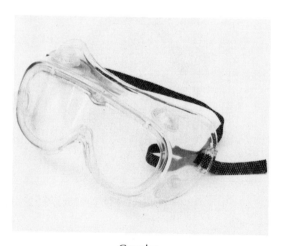

Goggles

Bench grinder

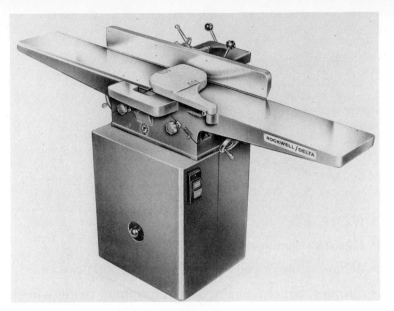

Jointer

Hammer

- *Hammers.* 13 ounces for finish, *16 ounces for general work.
- *Hearing protector,* if machine noise objectionable.
- *Honer,* tool.
- *Jointer,* 8-inch knives. 1½-hp. motor, totally enclosed.
- *Knife,* pocket, three-blade type. Putty or utility knife.
- *Lathe,* woodturning.

1220 Rotational Headband Hearing Protector

Utility knife

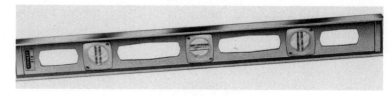

Level

- *Level,* 24-inch.
- *Mallet,* carver's 12–16-ounce.
- *Nail set,* *$\frac{1}{32}$, $\frac{2}{32}$, $\frac{3}{32}$, $\frac{4}{32}$.
- *Nails,* finish, *4d, *6d, 8d. 1-inch #18 brads, 1-pound box each.

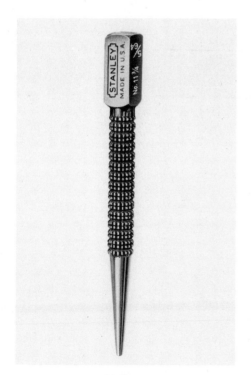

Nail set

Mallet, lignum vitae

• *Planer,* thickness. 12-inch knives. 2-hp. motor totally enclosed.

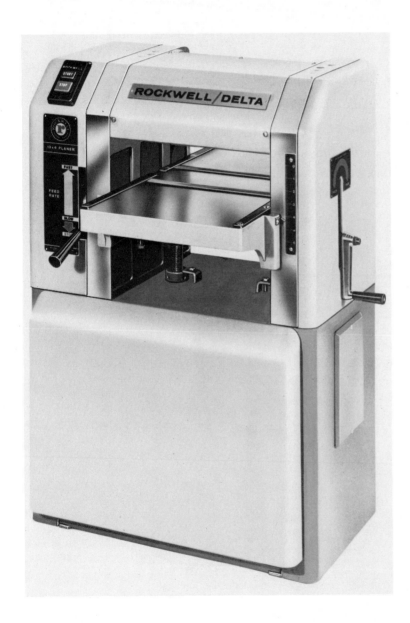

Thickness planer

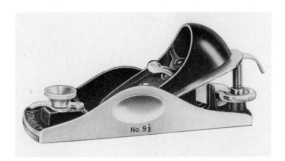

Block plane

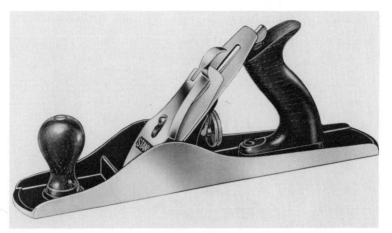

Jack plane

• *Planes.* *6-inch block. Compass plane. *14-inch jack. 22-inch jointer. 8½-inch rabbet or fillister. 7½-inch router. 9¾ inches smooth. Iron or wood.

• *Plastic wood or wood dough.* Natural, oak, light mahogany, walnut, one tube each.

Rabbet plane

Wood smooth plane

• *Router,* 8 amp. with ¼-, ⅜-, ½-inch radius cutters.
¼-, ½-inch groove cutters.

Router

Stationary belt sander

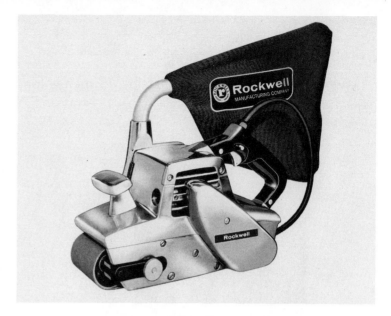

Belt sander

• *Sanders*. Belt 3" x 24" portable or 6" x 48" stationary. 60X, 80X belts, box of 10 each. Pneumatic drum with 2-, 3-inch-diameter x 9-inch-long drums. 80X, 120X sleeves, three of each size. Speed bloc finish sander.

Speed bloc
finish sander

Pneumatic
sander

- *Sanding block,* rubber or cork.
- *Sawhorses,* two, 32 inches high by 48 inches long. Can use Stanley brackets and 2 x 4 stock.

Sawhorse brackets

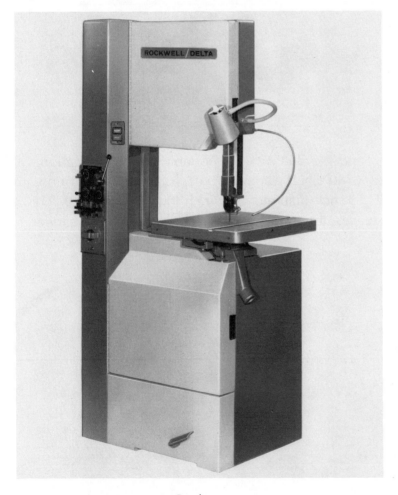

Band saw

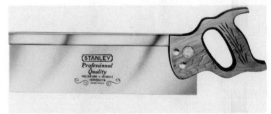

Backsaw

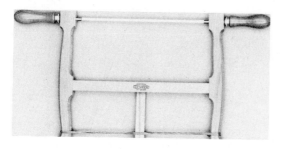

Bow saw

Crosscut saw

• *Saws.* Band, 14 inches with ¾-hp. totally enclosed motor. Backsaw. Offset backsaw. Bench saw, 10-inch tilting arbor with 1½-hp. totally enclosed motor with combination blade, dado set, planer blade. Bow saw.

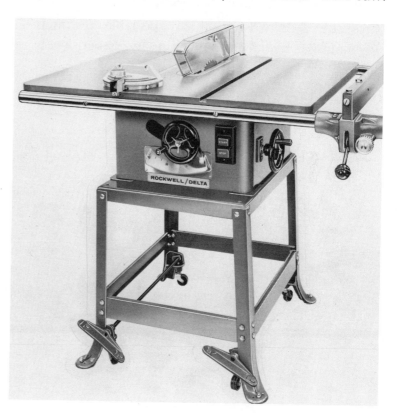

Bench saw

Saber saw

*Crosscut 12 point. Cut-off saw, portable, 6¾ inches.
Dovetail saw. Radial arm saw. Rip saw. Saber saw.

Portable cut-off saw

Double-handled cabinet scraper

• *Scrapers.* Double-handled. Gooseneck. Cabinet. Burnisher to complete the sharpening.

• *Screwdrivers,* oval handle for #6, #8, #10 wood screws. Screwdriver bits for brace also good.

• **Screws.* Flat or round head wood screws, #6, #8, #10; average length 1¼″, depends on thickness of stock involved.

• *Shaper,* single- or double-spindle.

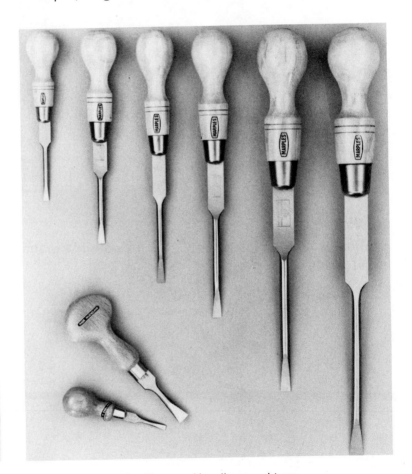

Oval boxwood handle screwdrivers

Ratchet screwdriver

- *Shoes*. Leather, work.
- *Shovel*, scoop type or large dustpan.
- *Spokeshave*, flat malleable iron.

Spokeshave

Framing square

- *Squares*, aluminum framing. *Combination try and miter.

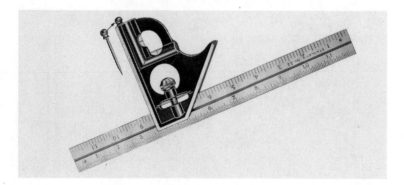

Combination square

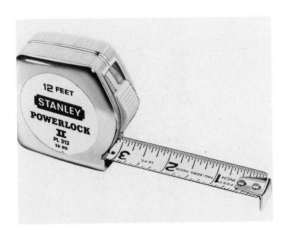

Steel measuring tape, clip-on type

Sharpening stone

- *Stone*, bench combination coarse and fine India. Stone oil or kerosene and motor oil mixed 50-50.
- *Tape*, 12-foot steel measuring.
- *Trash barrel* with cover.
- *Vise*, woodworking.

Woodworking Techniques

Never underestimate the cutting power of hand tools, particularly dull ones, on yourself. Some of the deepest cuts I've incurred have come from chisels. The dull edge tends to ricochet from the work surface instead of cutting in. Should you cut yourself, put pressure on the cut to stop bleeding, and apply Merthiolate and a bandage. If bleeding persists, see a doctor. A stitch or two, or the equivalent, promotes fast and infection-free healing, so if needed is well worth it. The best prevention against cuts is sharp tools and no fingers too near or ahead of the cutting edge. Never work when drowsy. Also, good tools and techniques go together. You can't expect to do a job well without knowing how to use your tools.

• *Abrasives*. Grit left in the wood from this operation dulls edge tools, therefore abrading should be the last step before finishing. Work with the grain and start with a coarse enough grit to remove tool marks. The lower the number, the coarser the grit. 60X or 80X is coarse enough usually, and should be used with a rubber cork or wood block to keep from digging in. Abrade through the grades to 120X for oil finish, 220X for urethane. Flint paper is all right on painted surfaces but dulls too fast to be good on wood, so stick to garnet, aluminum oxide, and silicon carbide.

• *Bench,* genuine woodworking. Keep the top flat, clean and smooth. Brush on a coat of boiled linseed oil and turpentine mixed half and half to finish the top and to keep glue from sticking to its surface. Clamp boards for planing with end vise and bench stops. Hold boards vertically in a face vise for cutting joints.

• *Brace and bits.* Use a jig (or guide) to keep hole at right angles to the surface. You may sight to a window mullion (a vertical pier between window panes).

• *Bevel, sliding.* Use to copy or transfer an angle. Particularly useful to hand cut a dovetail joint.

• *Box or chest for tools.* Necessary for tool storage and protection. Make or buy a box at least long enough for your rip and crosscut saws.

• *Chisels.* Make preliminary cuts in waste material first, then go back to scribed or marking gauge line. For production carving, check out pneumatic chiseling at your local supplier.

• *Clamps.* Alternate clamps top to bottom when clamping up tabletops or other flat surfaces.

• *Electric drill.* Use a drill 1/16 inch less than width of mortise to remove stock (the female member of the mortise and tenon joint) before chiseling if working by hand. Drill pilot holes for hardwood nailing. Use countersink or counterbore before drilling holes for screws unless you're using screw drills which do the whole operation at once.

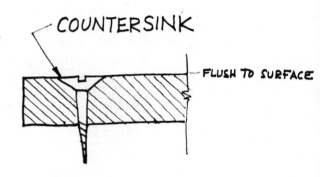

COUNTERSINK

FLUSH TO SURFACE

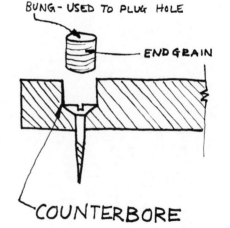

BUNG - USED TO PLUG HOLE

END GRAIN

COUNTERBORE

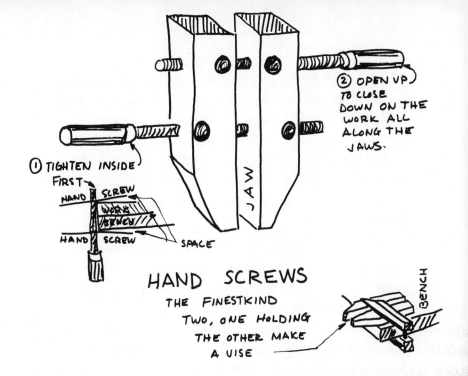

② OPEN UP TO CLOSE DOWN ON THE WORK ALL ALONG THE JAWS.

JAW

① TIGHTEN INSIDE FIRST

HAND SCREW
WORK
BENCH
HAND SCREW
SPACE

HAND SCREWS

THE FINESTKIND
TWO, ONE HOLDING
THE OTHER MAKE
A VISE

BENCH

BAR CLAMPS

FINEST KIND
FOR GLUING UP
TABLE TOPS + JOINERY

ALTERNATE OVER
AND UNDER TOPS
TO KEEP THE
WORK FLAT

• *Drill press.* Use for accurate drilling with jigs. Use drill 1/64 inch larger than dowel diameter for slide-fitting pegs for bookshelf supports, etc. A 5/16-inch hollow chisel bit which makes a "square hole" satisfies most furniture mortising requirements from stock ¾ to 1¼ inch thick. Can use brad point drills drilling about 1 inch diameter apart for wider mortises. Mortise speed is 2,800 rpm. Set the press at a lower speed for drilling or boring.

• *Files.* Use a bit file to sharpen your mortise bit and bits for brace. Sharpen inside of flute only — don't file bottom. Use a 12-inch mill single-cut flat file to file scraper blades before using the stone. It is also used in circular saw combination blades. The 12-inch Multikut is for flat wood filing and makes a fine cut from diamond file pattern. A 7-inch Slim Taper file is for sharpening handsaws, dado and planer blades. A Surform file is for wood shaping and makes the work easy.

• *Fire extinguisher.* Aim at base of fire. Tri-class means no risk of electric shock if it's an electrical fire. Call the fire department first in case your extinguisher runs out before the fire does.

• *Finishes.* Wood is less prone to checking and movement when sealed to the air with a surface or penetrating finish. A surface finish primarily protects the wood. A penetrating finish enhances the wood graining and deepens the color. Of course, there are combinations such as penetrating stains and sealer. I tend to keep finishing as simple as possible, using wood stains for toning or toning down contrasts in grain as required, but not appreciably changing the natural color. I do not mind the ripple of an orange peel effect on a surface and

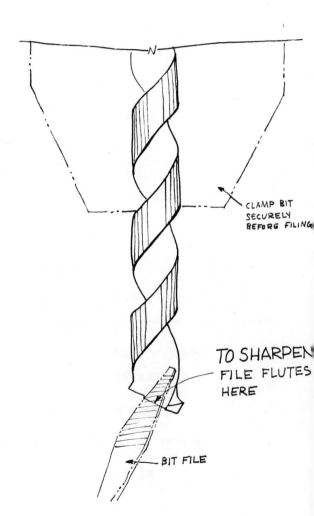

CLAMP BIT SECURELY BEFORE FILING

TO SHARPEN FILE FLUTES HERE

BIT FILE

don't look for the perfection of glass. I stay away from wood filler and allow the fact that wood is an organic, cellular and imperfect material to come through in the finish.

To apply linseed oil finish, mix the first application with steam-distilled turpentine 50-50. The only exception is a butcher block on which food will be prepared. In that case I use linseed oil without turpentine. Apply with a 2½-to-3-inch bristle brush to the surface which has been abraded with grades 60X, 80X, 100X, and 120X aluminum oxide sheets (known as abrading through 120X). Let the mixture stand from 4 to 6 hours, then abrade with 400X silicon carbide paper. Take a standard sheet and fold and tear carefully into quarters. Then fold the quarters into thirds and use in the palm of your hand. Abrade with the grain until you work up a paste. If the oil dries, add more. Wipe the paste first across the grain, then with the grain, using a folded cheesecloth pad. Let it dry at least twelve hours in a warm dry area like a boiler room. Test for dryness by rubbing a piece of newspaper on the surface to see if it draws oil. Apply the next coat of straight boiled oil by brush and let it stand about four hours. Then wet sand with 600X paper applying a small quantity of paraffin oil to the paper as a lubricant. Wipe off the paste as before and allow to dry. Linseed oil dries by oxidation so wipe as dry as possible in order to avoid a gummy surface and dispose of the cheesecloth in a covered container or underground to prevent spontaneous combustion. Heat can build up in the oil-soaked rags, causing them to ignite—I've seen it happen. Add another coat as with the second. When dry, a rubbing with paraffin oil, pure, will add luster to the finish. Use 600X paper with the grain and wipe off with the grain. To clean and wax an older linseed oil finish, mix the paraffin oil with steam-distilled turpentine 50-50, dab on a folded piece of 600X, and rub on. Add enough mixture to wet the surface. Let stand an hour and wipe off well with cheese-cloth. The residue will leave a low luster and not gum the surface.

The surface finish I prefer by far is urethane, widely marketed under a variety of brand names. You can buy either clear gloss or satin clear. The satin contains a dulling agent which tends to make the surface cloudy compared to the rubbed-down gloss, but it is more practical if you have a large wall area and don't want to rub down a large square footage. The gloss urethane is a marine finish, used on natural-finished boat trim. It also adapts well to a high-use surface like a floor, table or counter-top. Urethane dries and cures fast, is waterproof and does not waterspot like linseed oil. Urethane is a hard and durable finish, yet flexible with the wood, so it does not chip and crack like some varnishes and lacquers. Like all surface finishes, urethane ages and should be used fresh. When used partly cured and thick from the can, the finish could remain tacky. When dry, urethane has a slightly yellow color, tolerable on most woods in my opinion and particularly good on oak and mahogany. However I do not use urethane on American walnut because it blocks the full darkness and richness of the heartwood grain and yellows the gray sapwood objectionably. I mix dark walnut powder stain with linseed oil and apply it to tone down the sapwood areas. Sometimes I apply honey maple stain on pine to simulate aging.

• *Gauge, marking.* This tool will scribe a constant distance from an end or surface, so it's useful in hand joining or planing parallel to a surface.

• *Glasses or goggles* should be worn to protect your eyes from sawdust, etc., when using power tools or chisels.

• *Glue.* I use Titebond yellow glue most of the time. I've found it stronger than the white glue, although white will do. This aliphatic resin plastic glue sets in 10 minutes or so and dries satisfactorily in 45 minutes when clamped, less if in warm atmosphere. The glue is shock resistant and water resistant and does not dull tools as much as powder-mixed glues. Apply a film coat with a brush or a stick to each surface. You can stack the boards for a tabletop, having numbered them first with respect to position, and brush the glue on several edges at once. If the glue is too thick, a small amount of water will ease the work. This is a good time to wear your shop apron; use your sawhorses for the job. Lay the boards out flat on the sawhorses in order and apply a bar clamp; alternate sides every 16 inches or so. The glue will squeeze out and drip on the floor. Take a few scraps of wood and squeegee the glue off. Wipe off the remainder first with a damp dishrag, then with a dry rag. It's easier than waiting for the glue to dry on the surface. If you need more than 10 minutes to get your project together, use powder glue. I use Weldwood, which is commonly available. Add powder to a small amount of water and stir to a paste. Then add more to make a heavy cream consistency. Let stand a few minutes to dissolve any lumps. Apply and remove the excess as above. Weldwood takes about ½ hour to set and about 6 hours to dry when clamped. It is more brittle than Titebond and is water resistant, but it's subject to shelf age. If it's over a year old it may set quickly when mixed. If this happens get new glue.

Because of the high porosity of the end grain, gluing is only 50 percent as effective there as it is on long-grain surfaces except when an epoxy is used. When joining, therefore, use glue on the long grain only and the joint will be quite strong enough. On dowel joints, where about half the surface is end grain, you'll apply glue on both the end and long grains and still not have the holding power of the mortise and tenon. No doubt you've seen wobbly chair and table legs—evidence of this weaker joint.

For marine or exterior application use waterproof or epoxy glue, available at marine supply or hardware stores. These glues are catalyst and resin types, mixed at assembly. They set in about ½ hour and dry in about 24. Urethane is adequate protection for water-resistant glues in interior areas.

The business of glue brings to mind some of my youthful experience. I had an early regard for the way walnut shells fit quite well together if you shucked them carefully and refitted them. I was in the airplane glue stage then, but didn't like the way it kept sticking to my hands. I found some yellow glue one day and was pleased at how easily it washed off, so I thought it would do a pretty neat job gluing the walnut shells I collected back together. Dabbing the glue on both surfaces, holding the shells for a few minutes, and then wiping them off gave me a nice little pile of recycled walnuts. I used to go into convulsions recalling the Old Man's

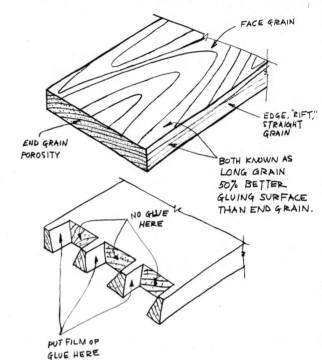

FACE GRAIN

EDGE, "RIFT," STRAIGHT GRAIN

END GRAIN POROSITY

BOTH KNOWN AS LONG GRAIN 50% BETTER GLUING SURFACE THAN END GRAIN.

NO GLUE HERE

PUT FILM OF GLUE HERE

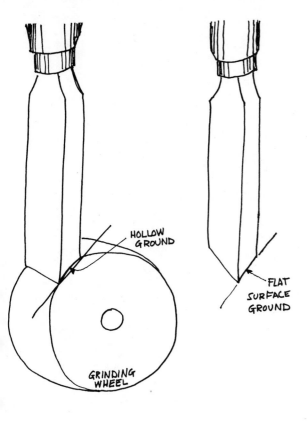

HOLLOW GROUND

FLAT SURFACE GROUND

GRINDING WHEEL

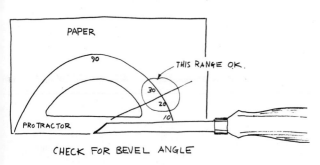

PAPER

90

THIS RANGE OK.

30

20

10

PROTRACTOR

CHECK FOR BEVEL ANGLE

expression as he opened countless numbers of these re-worked specimens and at the same time trying to engage in a profound conversation. I can still hear the nut-cracker.

• *Grinder, bench.* I prefer a hollow ground bevel on my plane irons and chisels as opposed to the milled flat bevel. You need to lift off this milled flat bevel to complete the sharpening on your bench stone, and if you lift it off too far you can roll the cutting edge so you're dulling instead of sharpening your tool. The hollow ground bevel can locate the front and back edges of the bevel on your bench stone, the middle being concave from conforming to the circumference of the 6-to-12-inch-diameter grinding wheel. Because the hollow ground bevel gives a more positive location on the bench stone to complete the sharpening, I use it when needed.

The hand grinding wheel I use is plenty adequate for the job. Get one with good bearings so the wheel doesn't wobble from side to side. Hand grinders are no longer commonly available, though you may be able to special order one from your hardware store or find a used one. Their main advantage over power-driven grinders is a lower speed, and as a result, no burning of the tool edge. Burning causes loss of the temper and the ability of the tool to hold an edge. You can avoid overheating by dipping the edge frequently in a can of water.

The grinder has a tool holder to maintain the desired bevel angle on your tools; 30 degrees is about right. You could have 25 degrees for soft wood, so as to shear the wood rather than mash it. Check your bevel angle by outlining it on paper and measuring it with a pro-tractor. If it's a few degrees off, bear it in mind when you set the tool holder. To set the tool holder to the bevel angle, loosen the adjustment nut and, with the iron or chisel on the holder, set the iron tangentially to the wheel at the center of the bevel and tighten the nut again, checking that your alignment is still main-tained. Do this by eye. A few degrees one way or the other doesn't matter. Learn to rely on your eye. It may well be the best gauge you'll ever have; likewise your hands are the best tools. Everything else is at best a good accessory. If you find your tools dulling quickly in hardwood, increase the bevel angle to about 35 degrees.

To grind the iron or chisel, hold it firmly on the tool rest and against the grinding wheel, but do not jam or feed in the edge or you'll burn it. Also move the tool back and forth evenly across the stone. The edge should be square to the length and the corners of a plane iron rounded to about 1/32-inch radius, to prevent digging into your board later. The best grinding wheel I've come across is made of aluminum oxide which wears evenly as used, maintaining a clean surface; it also runs cooler than the conventional carborundum. Have a dressing stick of silicon carbide to go with your wheel. When held in firm position on the tool holder, the stick will abrade high spots on the wheel with light contact. The grinding is complete if the bevel angle is uniform and the cutting edge does not shine when held up to a strong light source. Glasses, goggles or a guard on the machine will protect your eyes from sparks.

The best grinding system consists of an abrasive belt running around two wheels. This setup provides an

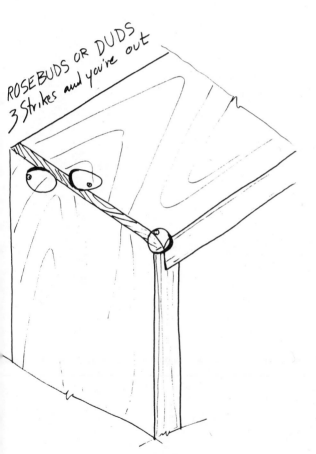

ROSEBUDS OR DUDS
3 Strikes and you're out

adequate abrading surface, and it's easy to replace the belt. You can build your own grinding system. On the market they are more than six times the cost of stone grinders. On the other hand, maybe they are that much better, because with a buffing wheel and abrasive compound you can do away with a bench sharpening stone. I personally don't use it but the results I've seen are superior.

• *Hammers.* For heavy-duty jobs a 16-ounce hammer with a rubber grip over steel or fiberglas absorbs the shock better than wood. A 13-ounce hammer with an ash or hickory handle is fine for finish work. Rub it down with linseed oil. Hold the hammer at the end of the handle and snap your wrist to drive a nail. This lets the weight of the hammer do the work and maintains alignment with the nail so you don't leave any rosebuds or souvenirs. I remember my early carpentry days on a floor job. The carpenters kept getting ahead of me on nailing so I thought I'd try a big swing, more like a pitcher. After a while I noticed the carpenters looking at me with a slightly pained look. They had noticed the rosebuds. I hadn't hit the nail much but you could see where I'd been. So maintain alignment and be a turtle for a while. Remember the fable. Unless you intend to angle them, start nails upright—and use your eye to check them. Hold the nail with your thumb and index finger to start and then get your fingers out of the way. (If you forget, the hammer will remind you so you won't forget as often.) In cabinet work it is desirable to set the finish nails below the surface and cover them with plastic wood, wood dough, wax crayon or shellac sticks on visible surfaces. Drive the nail to within ⅛ inch of the surface, then use the nail set that will fit in the cup of the finish nail head or the $\frac{1}{32}$-inch size. Hold the nail set in line with the nail and pound firmly on the head. Several hits from the hammer set the nail. For production nailing, look at a pneumatic stapler at your local supply.

• *Hands, your*. Hand cleaner and a tube of lanolin will keep your hands free of grit and the skin from drying out, helps prevent blisters and soothes the ones you may already have.

• *Hearing protector*. This earmuff-design protector is not a toy and only a damn fool will make merry of how it looks. They are available at welding suppliers and will prevent your hearing from deteriorating. Your hearing ability can be dangerously affected by the noise of power tools if you do not wear a protector. When I couldn't hear the birds sing any more I took action. (The cardinal is my idea of a bird and someday I may come back as one. So if you see one planing boards for his nest some day you'll know who it is. Especially if he has on a hearing protector.) Incidentally, I've enjoyed hearing the birds since I've been wearing the hearing protector and notice much less fatigue, having cut down on the noise pollution.

• *Honer, tool*. Use it as a jig or fixture to maintain a constant bevel angle when using the bench stone. The universal ball bearing on the bottom of the clamp-on bracket avoids any limitations in the sharpening pattern.

• *Jointer*, 8-inch knives, 1½-hp. motor, totally enclosed. This machine will dress an edge or surface true enough to butt together with another piece likewise dressed for

WHAT YOU SHOULD KNOW ABOUT NOISE AND HEARING

Before you make any decisions about hearing protection you should be aware of certain facts.

Loud noise can cause permanent hearing loss.

The loudness (or intensity) is measured in decibels (dB) with a *Sound Level Meter*, and because the A scale on the meter is used, the readings are expressed in dBA.

Harzardous noise can be divided into 2 groups:

MODERATE NOISE 90 - 110 dBA

HIGH NOISE, over 110 dBA

Damage to hearing accelerates as noise gets louder, so the government limits the time that an unprotected worker can be exposed to various noise levels:

Duration Per Day (hours)	Noise Level (dBA)
8	90
6	92
4	95
3	97
2	100
1½	102
1	105
½	110
¼	115

Because decibels are *logarithmic* units an increase of a few decibels represents a much bigger jump than you might expect.

For example, a 10 decibel noise is 10 times more intense than 1 decibel, but 20 decibels is 100 times more intense than 1 decibel, 30 decibels is 1,000 times more intense than 1, and so on.

Without an accurate sound level survey, you can't be certain that your plant doesn't have hazardous noise. But here's a good rule of thumb:

If your employees must raise their voices to be heard by someone less than 2 feet away, chances are they need hearing protection.

TYPICAL SOUND LEVELS

	DECIBELS		DECIBELS
Rocket Launching Pad	180	Hydraulic Press	85
Jet Aircraft	140	Can Mfg Plant	100
Gunshot Blast	140	Subway	90
Riveting Steel Tank	130	Computer Card Verifier	85
Car Horn	120	Noisy Diner	80
Sandblasting	112	Office Tabulator	80
Woodworking Shop	100	Busy Traffic	75
Punch Press	100	Conversational Speech	66
Pneumatic Drill	100	Average Home	50
Boiler Shop	100	Rustling Leaves	10

a good glue joint. The stock is placed on the infeed table, usually set 1/16 inch lower than the cutter head knives. The outfeed table is set at a tangent to the highest point in the knife arc. If the surface is milled convex, the outfeed table is too high, and the work could hit the edge of the outfeed table instead of passing over it. The outfeed is too low if the surface is clipped or snipped at the end. Outfeed adjustment is set fairly easily by hand-turning the cutter head by pulling on the belt to the motor while holding a piece of stock on the outfeed and projecting over the cutter. When the knives turn counterclockwise they just want to kiss the piece of wood. If they lift it you're too low. Disconnect the power before adjustment. This procedure is also useful to set the knives in the cutter head after removal for grinding. The grinding is done at a sharpening shop to keep them balanced and flat. The knives can be touched up on a bench stone or honed in place on the cutter head. I prefer removing the cutters because I can get them sharper that way. The 8-inch knife is the minimum practical size for surface work. The planer then dresses the opposite side parallel. The fence on the jointer is used for right-angle or bevel work. So, before selecting a jointer, examine the fence for straightness at least by eye and note the adjustment mechanism for rigidity when set. You shouldn't be able to move it easily when tight, and it should have positive adjustable stops for 45 and 90 degrees. The planer and jointer enable you to buy stock rough. When ready, you do the milling. A thousand board-feet later it will be paid for and you'll be pleased the stock wasn't sitting around dressed and beginning to warp. Of course in carpentry work, warping isn't the very real problem it is in cabinetry.

To joint the board select the concave surface. Check for grit and metal, and cut back the ends. If the board has twist of ¼ inch or so you may want to rip it (cut it to width) or cut it an inch over the finished length to avoid losing thickness. I rip the stock if I'm going to lose over ¼ inch thickness. Put paraffin wax on the infeed and outfeed tables before starting up. Feed the stock steadily, with the grain running toward you as much as possible; don't rock or it won't be flat. As the stock passes over the knives, put one hand over the outfeed table and go hand over hand until the stock has all passed the cutters. If the stock is over six feet long you'll need a table support in addition to the outfeed table. There is no need to pass your hands directly over the cutters, although I do it on 2-inch-thick stock. On thin stock, use another piece with a cleat on the bottom and a handle. For safety I don't joint stock under ½ inch thick or stock that is unsound, cracked or checked through. I also won't joint cedar, which splits if you talk to it the wrong way.

• *Knife, pocket.* Keep it sharp by drawing each side of the blade alternately over the rough, then fine, side of your bench stone. The fine side is adequate for touching up. The knife is used as a scribe and is more accurate and precise than a pencil in marking off hand-cut dovetail joints, mortises and lengths.

• *Lathe, woodturning.* Turning is a special woodworking technique that produces rounds or offset rounds and ovals; it is used in making bowls, frames, chair spindles and legs, and round tabletops (although the latter can be

LATHE

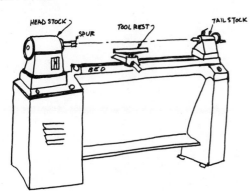

HEAD STOCK   SPUR   TOOL REST   BED   TAIL STOCK

produced on a shaper or a router, or hand-planed from the band saw cut).

There are two types of turning: long turning along the bed of the lathe, using both the head stock and tail stock; and face plate turning at right angles to the bed for larger diameters. Turning tools are required; they are used with a tool rest at all times. Goggles or glasses should be worn. You generally work from a section plan and check dimensions with a caliper as you go. Abrading is done with the stock in place on the lathe and turning. I'm not a lathe man myself because of the tremendous commercial production of turnings that are done on automatic lathes in colonial furniture of the Gardner, Massachusetts, ilk. I tend toward rounding with the router, hand planing, and Surform filing. However, the lathe does have validity for small quantities of turnings and it is possible to impart your design on lathe work, be it round or oval.

• *Level, 24-inch.* This is a good size for general horizontal and vertical checks on built-ins or construction. Examine the vials when buying. They should be firmly cemented in place and the bubble should be as long as the distance between the scribe lines for accurate reading. Check for identical readings on each side as an indication of accuracy. Use it with care and don't drop or jam the level against a surface, as this can cause misalignment and loss of accuracy. A well-made cabinet looks none too good installed cockeyed, so keep the level handy for frequent on-the-job checking.

• *Mallet, 13-ounce carver's.* It can be turned on a lathe or bought. I prefer it to the carpenter's square face be-

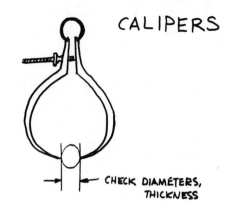

CALIPERS

CHECK DIAMETERS, THICKNESS

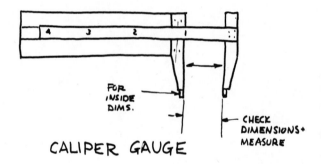

CALIPER GAUGE

FOR INSIDE DIMS.

CHECK DIMENSIONS + MEASURE

cause alignment isn't as critical when driving the chisel. When joining I tend to watch where the edge of the chisel is cutting rather than the handle or the mallet, so I want something that works easily. As with the hammer, hold the mallet at the end of its handle and snap your wrist to operate.

• *Motors, electric.* I've found over the years that dust can cause motor failure, which costs time, money and causes aggravation. It's better to buy sealed or totally enclosed motors. The initial additional cost will be cheaper in the long run than paying for repairs on partially enclosed models. The totally enclosed motor cools with air fanned over the jacket, whereas the partially enclosed motor draws air through the motor. Check the specifications with care before buying one.

• *Nail set.* Unless you want souvenirs of where you've been, you should own this inexpensive hand tool. (See illustration of rosebuds or duds on page 43.) Especially handy is the 1/32-inch set, because it leaves the smallest hole when using the small #18 wire brad.

• *Nails, finish,* 4d, 6d, 8d; brads, 1-inch #18. One 1-pound box each. Use these small round-head nails in place of the common large head in exposed areas on cabinets because they hold reasonably well and are easily covered over when set. 4d, 6d, 8d nails are 1½, 2, and 2½ inches long, respectively. The ''d'' means penny, which originally referred to cost per hundred. They're still quite cheap, so have 4d and 6d nails available for plywood rabbet joints on cabinets and 8d to attach casings, chair rails and other wall trim. Space nails evenly; if close to an edge or end use 4d nails.

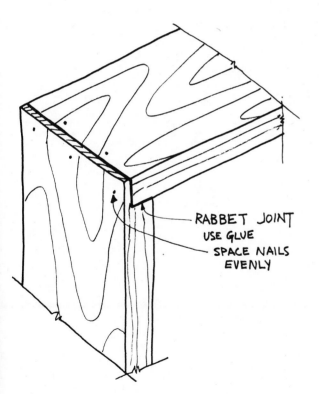

RABBET JOINT
USE GLUE
SPACE NAILS
EVENLY

Plain steel is all right for interior work. On exterior use galvanized steel. Always use glue with the nails on cabinets. Use the 1-inch brads on small work like spice shelves or noteboxes when the stock is ½ or ¼ inch thick. Number 18 is the smallest wire gauge commonly available; I recommend it since it's the least likely to split the stock.

• *Planer, thickness, 12-inch knives, 2 hp. motor fully enclosed.* This machine will give you independence from the planing mill for most jobs. 12 inches is a small-capacity machine but large enough for most boards. Wider stock can either be ripped and glued back, hand planed, or milled elsewhere. To use the planer, place the jointed surface down on the infeed table with the grain running toward you. The corrugated overhead roller will grab the board and feed it into the cutters. You receive the job on the other side labor-free. While it is not necessary to have a vacuum attachment and a hood over the cutters to remove the shavings with this machine, it greatly reduces the dust. I let the shavings and dust go and clean up afterward—but I don't run it all day long either. Wear a respirator to keep from breathing in too much dust. A cap may do you some good, too. The average cut on the planer is 1/16 to 1/8 inch. Measure the thickness of your stock and set the table 1/8 inch less to start. Apply paraffin to the infeed and out-feed tables before turning on the motor. Never use your hands to clear away chips on the machine while it's running or before it has stopped. It will mill your fingers as clean as you want to get. Note the location of the clutch to stop the infeed in an emergency, such as jamming the machine from too heavy a cut. In this case throw the clutch out and back the table down a turn. Then you can engage the clutch again. Take care not to wear loose clothing that can catch on the rough-sawn board and be dragged into the planer. Also, check your stock for grit, pebbles and steel; they can ruin the knives. The commonly used domestic stock when clean won't work the knives hard. However, some of the exotic imports, like teak, will level your knives in a few boards due to their heavy mineral content. If you must work a quantity of teak let someone else mill it and tear his hair out. A mill working teak will have a cutting head chock full of carbide cutters with a silicon carbide grinding wheel attachment. A small quantity of teak is no problem at all with your hand planes. Try it and be pleasantly surprised.

The adjustments on a planer are relevant to good performance and should be noted when buying any machine, new or used. The acme screw movement, which raises and lowers the table should run free and parallel to the cutter. Keep the screws cleaned and lightly oiled. To check that the table is parallel to the knives, disconnect the power and position the table with a block of wood on one side so that it just makes contact with the knives. Now carefully remove the block and try it on the other side of the table to see if it makes contact with the knives. If the block jams into the knives, slack off on the collar on the acme screws. If the block rides free under the knives, advance the collar to take up the difference. The parallel cut is important to save work in matching up boards when gluing.

The stock is drawn into and through the planer by a corrugated infeed roller and a smooth outfeed roller set about 1/32 inch below the arc of the knives. If it were higher, the stock wouldn't be drawn in at the correct setting to mill 1/16 to 1/8 inch. If lower, the rollers would chew up your stock. Adjustment nuts are on top, directly over the rollers. Keep the rollers clean. Turpentine and a rag is what I use, with the power off, of course. The chipbreaker, directly behind the knives, also is best set 1/32 inch below the arc of the knives to prevent chipping the grain. If it is too low, however, the stock will drag on it or be jammed. The two idler rollers should be about 1/64 inch above and parallel to the table. They should turn when a board passes over them on the table but should not perceptibly lift the board. The adjustment nuts are directly under the rollers. The planer has grease fittings on the upper rollers and calls for grease about every ten hours of operation time to prevent wear on the bearings. Be familiar with the instruction manual for the machine you buy. Always keep the knives sharp. You can touch up some, honing the knives on the machine with the power supply disconnected. If the knives are chipped, slack off the nuts on the cutter shims, carefully remove the knives, wrap them in heavy paper, and take them to a reliable sharpening service for precision grinding. Dull knives pound the daylight out of the machine and leave a pounded glossy finish on your stock. Before removing the knives, set a block that just makes contact with them; and leave the block as a check that the knives are even and parallel to the table before fully tightening up on the cutter shims when replacing the knives. Handle the razor-sharp knives with care and never run your finger over the edge. Have the power disconnected and rotate the

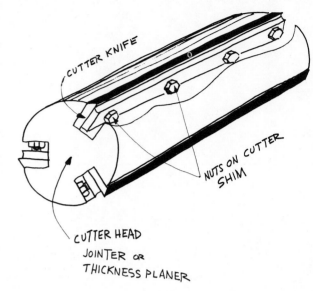

CUTTER KNIFE

NUTS ON CUTTER SHIM

CUTTER HEAD
JOINTER or
THICKNESS PLANER

cutter head by pulling on the motor belts when checking the knife adjustment with the block.

• *Planes, 6-inch block.* The block plane is the correct choice in the family of planes for end-grain work like smoothing or bringing into square because the cutter or plane iron is at a relatively low angle to the base or bed of the plane. This allows for a clean cut across the wood fibers, the hardest surface of a board. The block plane I use is Stanley U.S.A. number 60½. The angle of the iron on this model is about 20 degrees. To work efficiently, the plane must be sharp—as should all edge tools. If it has not been sharpened recently, the iron should be removed and checked for sharpness as follows. Hold the plane in one hand with the cutting edge of the iron forward. Then slide the retaining lever to the left on the cap (the casting directly on top of the iron). Then slide the cap back until the retaining machine screw fits through the hole in the cap. Lift off the cap and then the iron. Hold the iron up to a strong light source to see if there's any shine on the edge to indicate dullness (see Grinder above and Stones below). If sharpening is not needed, reassemble the plane carefully, taking care not to jam the sharp edge against metal.

The bevel is up and the in-out adjustment lug fits into grooves in the iron. The iron should be adjusted parallel to the bed either by moving the lever directly under it or by tapping it lightly with a hammer. Also, the iron must project slightly below the bed. The iron is usually advanced by turning the knurled adjustment screw at the back of the plane clockwise and retracted by turning it counterclockwise. Fractional turns make the difference between a light and heavy cut. To plane, one hand applies pressure down or against the stock in front while the hand behind pushes. Paraffin on the base reduces the friction noticeably. There is no shaving on end-grain work as with long-grain, even when the cutter is sharp, as the cohesion here is negligible. When squaring up is necessary after a saw cut, check first with a combination square to find the high spot. Concentrate on shaving this down. Plane from edge to center, as planing forward over an edge will splinter the wood. As the plane cuts only forward, lift it off to avoid dulling the iron dragging it over the surface. A few cuts in the right area are often all that's needed. Check again with your combination square to avoid overcutting. A pencil line to work up to also helps prevent taking off too much. On exposed edges and corners it's a good practice to break (take the sharp edge off) the edge to avoid splinters. The block plane is good here for either a chamfer or rounded edge before abrading.

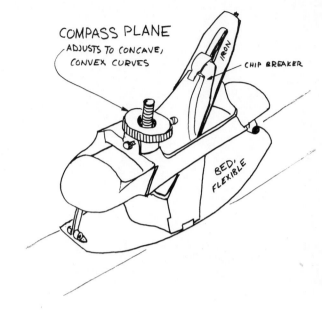

COMPASS PLANE
ADJUSTS TO CONCAVE, CONVEX CURVES
IRON
CHIP BREAKER
BED FLEXIBLE

• *A compass plane* is used for hand planing over a continuous curve because the bed is adjustable. Have the bed slightly more curved than the surface you are planing so it will be sure to make contact with the stock. The iron should be set for a light cut. Apply downward as well as forward pressure to operate it. I use this plane most on curved rails and rockers in chair work. It's also useful in making jigs for production. Note that the bevel of the plane iron is down and a chipbreaker is screwed to the iron on the side opposite the bevel. The edge of the chipbreaker should be about 1/32 inch from the edge of the iron. Slide the chipbreaker carefully into position; don't run over the edge, as this dulls it. Hand tighten the holddown screw on the chipbreaker; then

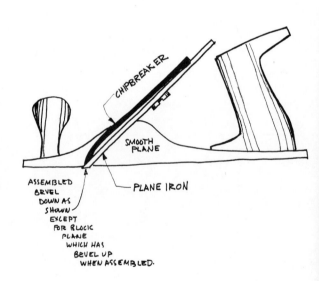

CHIPBREAKER
SMOOTH PLANE
PLANE IRON
ASSEMBLED BEVEL DOWN AS SHOWN EXCEPT FOR BLOCK PLANE WHICH HAS BEVEL UP WHEN ASSEMBLED.

use the front edge of the cap as a screwdriver to tighten completely. Note that the in-out adjustment lug fits into the slot in the chipbreaker. Also note the lateral adjustment lever under the iron. Check for squareness or work to a line.

• *A jack plane, 14-inch,* is the all-around carpenter's choice because it's medium-sized and can do most flat planing operations reasonably well. I use it as a scaled-down jointer plane on small surfaces and tables. It's the first plane I bought. The adjustments are the same as for the compass plane described above. Also see Grinding above and Stone sharpening below. To make flush glued-up boards or joints, work the high parts first and work toward the center on an angle (or shear cut) at about 45 degrees. This will minimize tearing the grain and splintering on edges. Tip your plane at a 45-degree angle and use the bottom edge as a guide for flatness. If the grain picks up or raises, reverse your angle of work or work in an oval rather than straight pattern. Finish by planing with the grain. A smooth plane is good on this part and is what I use. See Smooth plane. Put paraffin on the bed of the plane as you work and set the plane on its side when not in use to avoid chipping the iron on any metal. See Jointer plane below for preparing edges or surface to glue up.

• *Jointer plane, 22-inch.* The long bed of the jointer plane guarantees a flatter surface over a longer length than that of the shorter jack plane. So when gluing boards over five feet, this is the hand plane to use. Sharpening and adjustments are the same as for the compass and jack planes above. For sharpening, see Grinding above and Stone sharpening below. To prepare boards for gluing with the jointer plane, proceed as follows.

Dress the stock on two surfaces at least enough to see the grain pattern and to ensure that the surfaces are parallel to each other. First plane *across* the grain of one surface at about a 45-degree angle (known as a skew cut), then plane *with* the grain. Then use your marking gauge to scribe off a uniform thickness. Now plane the other surface the same way. This process will do for a small quantity of rough-sawn hardwood. For a larger amount have it milled, or see Jointer and Planer above, or buy pine already dressed at a lumberyard. Lay the boards out on sawhorses with the inside surface up. This is the surface toward the center of the tree, so the annual growth rings at the end of the board are cupped or concave. This means the boards will all have a tendency to warp in the same direction, that is, curling toward the center. It's easier to hold down a top glued in this manner than it is if the boards curl alternately. Look for a pleasing arrangement of the boards, preferably with the grain running in the same direction. I look for some kind of balance or symmetry, except in edge or rift (straight-grained) sawn stock where the pattern is fairly uniform. Number the edges of the boards on the top face. Now clamp one board with an edge to be jointed between benchstops or in a vise. Dress the edge square to the numbered surface. Use your combination square to check. The jointer plane should be set for a light cut. You should get a shaving the full width of the edge along the whole length as you work. To keep the cut flat, push down on the front when you start and maintain pressure against the wood all along the cut, then ease up at the

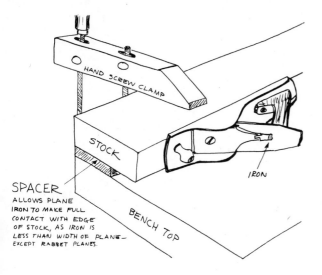

HAND SCREW CLAMP

STOCK

IRON

SPACER
ALLOWS PLANE
IRON TO MAKE FULL
CONTACT WITH EDGE
OF STOCK, AS IRON IS
LESS THAN WIDTH OF PLANE—
EXCEPT RABBET PLANES.

BENCH TOP

far end so as not to clip or snip it low. Sight along the edge for straightness and check carefully for squareness. Then take a few shavings from the center of the edge. Start the iron gradually a few inches in and lift off a few inches from the far end. Then take another cut or two a few inches inside the first cut. This procedure will prevent checking at the ends by leaving more stock to allow for shrinkage. With two edges joined and resting against each other the ends will touch, leaving a bit of daylight in the middle. Check that the boards draw up tight with no glue before gluing (see Glue). If your boards come from the lumberyard, check them for straightness and squareness and correct if needed. Then take a few shavings from the middle, as above. If the boards have any rock in them check for the high point with your square before planing; concentrate on the high spot only.

You can also clamp the board to be jointed against a smooth flat surface with a ½-inch or thicker spacer board set back about ¼ inch from the edge, and dressed parallel on two surfaces. Your jointer plane then works on its side, which maintains the square alignment needed. I use this method of jointing with stock ¼ to 1½ inches thick if the jointer is not available and the quantity is small. Be sure to check your jointer plane for squareness, edge to bottom; this can be corrected by precision grinding at a machine shop. Or you can alternate your board surfaces up and down to cancel out the variance from a right angle, as I do. The wood bed jointer plane is quite good because the wedge set can hold the iron with more pressure over a greater area than the adjustment mechanism described above, provided the plane is handled carefully and not jarred when set down.

The wood jointer plane is a bench tool. It doesn't travel to the job as well as its cast-iron counterpart. The adjustment is set by placing the iron and chipbreaker in position flush and parallel to the bottom of the plane and inserting the wedge by hand to hold this position. Then tap the wedge several times with a hammer to set it. Then try the plane for evenness and lightness of cut. Tap the iron lightly on top to increase the cut. To retract the plane iron on wooden planes, tap the metal striking knob with your hammer. The knob is usually in front of the iron on jointer planes and behind the iron on smooth planes. There are several advantages to the wood plane; it doesn't rust too much or discolor the wood, and if it's not perfectly straight or square you can correct it with another plane. Also, you can modify the bed if you want to plane to a fixed pattern, as in making saddle seats for chairs. About the only disadvantage is that the adjustment of the iron can take more time than the screw adjustment type. Because of the time involved, I prefer the screw adjustment type, though it's somehow esthetically appealing to use wood on wood and there's less chance of bruising your stock.

• *Rabbet or fillister plane, 8½-inch.* This hand tool will cut rabbet joints for bookcases and cabinets on both the frame and setting in the back. Set the double-arm fence to the thickness of the stock you want to let in and set the depth gauge for ⅔ the thickness. If cutting across the grain, allow the hardened steel spur to project below the bottom of the plane to score the wood as you plane. The spur requires filing on the bevel side, then

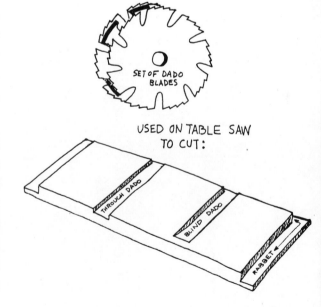

SET OF DADO BLADES

USED ON TABLE SAW TO CUT:

THROUGH DADO

BLIND DADO

RABBET

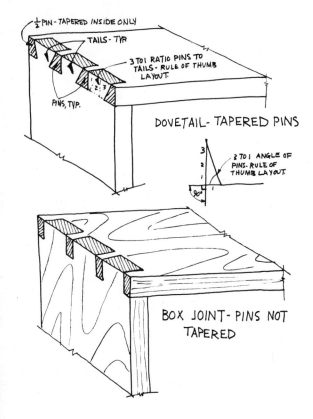

½ PIN - TAPERED INSIDE ONLY

TAILS - TYP.

3 TO 1 RATIO PINS TO TAILS - RULE OF THUMB LAYOUT.

PINS, TYP.

2 : 3

DOVETAIL - TAPERED PINS

3
2
1

3 TO 1 ANGLE OF PINS. RULE OF THUMB LAYOUT.

90°

BOX JOINT - PINS NOT TAPERED

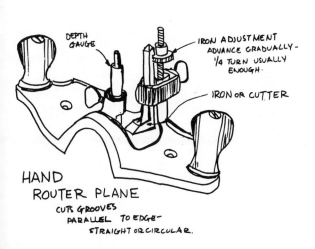

DEPTH GAUGE

IRON ADJUSTMENT ADVANCE GRADUALLY - ¼ TURN USUALLY ENOUGH.

IRON OR CUTTER

HAND ROUTER PLANE

CUTS GROOVES PARALLEL TO EDGE - STRAIGHT OR CIRCULAR.

honing on your bench stone so that you have a sharp and acute edge to slice clean when working across the grain. The iron should be sharpened square to the edge and straight with no curved or rounded corners. Adjust the iron for a light cut to start. Your plane may have two locations for the iron. The forward gets into corners. It's simpler to execute designs that use through-rabbet cuts so you don't need to hand rout or chisel the blind ends by keeping end and edge rabbets the same depth. Blind rabbet cuts must be made to let in the back on cabinets with box or through-dovetail joints. The rabbet plane is a common carpenter's tool. If you've never used one, you may be pleasantly surprised how easily and quickly a rabbet can be cut along a piece of pine. Certainly this plane is an inexpensive solution for a limited amount of this work compared to the cost of power tools like the router or even table saw and dado-set blades.

• *Router plane, 7½-inch.* The router plane allows you to cut grooves *inboard* (as opposed to on the edge) and works reasonably well from curved edges. It usually comes with ¼- and ½-inch cutters, adjusted to the work by screw feed. Set the fence so the cutter is about ¼ inch in from the edge. Use the flat side of the fence for a straight cut, the indented side for a curved one. Begin with the cutter flush to the bottom of the bed and turn the knurled adjustment clockwise until you make a light cut. The cutter is held in position by a clamp collar with a thumbscrew that should be set as low as it can go on the stud for maximum rigidity of the cutter. First slack off on the thumbscrew before making the adjustment then tighten up again. This is more time-consuming than using the power router, but if you've only a few grooves to cut for drawer bottoms, this is the inexpensive way to do it yourself. When routing across the grain, dadoing, make a few saw cuts on the waste side of the line and work in from each edge first with a flat chisel. No fence is needed, but work carefully to avoid riding over the saw cut and splintering. Make the saw cut the full depth of the dado as scored with the marking gauge.

The depth gauge works with the thin end down in its housing in front of the router. With the thin end on the surface of your work and the thumbscrew on the housing slacked off allowing the gauge to run free, slide the shoe up on the depth gauge the desired depth of the groove and tighten the shoe thumbscrew at this setting. The depth gauge will ride in the groove as you cut and when the shoe falls on the housing you will be at the desired depth. The depth gauge and shoe also serve independent of the router to check the depth of mortises. The shoe can also be set flush or a hair below the bottom of the plane for additional support when routing.

I use the hand router mostly as a supplement to a dado cut from the table saw. At the point where the ends of the dado cut come flush to the surface, I first cut down square with a flat bench chisel. Then I can take out the remaining stock to the bottom of the dado in a few heavy cuts. This often applies to grooves for drawer bottoms. The hand router is also good for correcting groove depth variance when cutting across warped stock. If your groove is at least ½ inch wide and you want it smooth, such as for drawer runners, use the smoothing diamond-point cutter that cuts on a shear for best results.

• *Smooth plane, 9¾-inch.* Used on surfaces for smoothing after using the jack or jointer planes. Round the corners of the iron to prevent digging in and use a light cut and short strokes. Work with the grain. You'll then be ready for scraping or sanding.

• *Plastic wood or wood dough* is a quick-drying lacquer-base wood filler that's good for filling in finished nail holes and around knots and small imperfections in the grain. Buy it in tubes rather than in cans for the wood you're using as it keeps better this way. Light woods take natural color. Apply with a putty knife and allow ten minutes for it to dry before sanding. It shrinks when drying, so apply a little extra. Shellac sticks are a better filler. Burn the stick with the flame from a match and let the melted portion drip into the cavity or holes you want filled. Let the shellac harden before sanding. Wax crayons can also fill small holes. Apply after finishing with a matching color. If the wood is to be painted, vinyl spackle is as good as anything; there's both an interior and exterior preparation available.

• *Router, 8 amp.,* with ¼-, ⅜-, ½-inch radius cutters, and ¼-, ½-inch groove cutters. Light milling can be done with a smaller router than this one, but then you begin to stall and chatter on the heavier operations, like routing out a tray. Whether using a template or routing free form on a tray, stay an inch or so inboard of your final perimeter and blend the edges to the routed depth with your gouge chisels, starting with a more curved one and working toward the flat one. The router depth of cut should not exceed ³⁄₁₆ inch—at least, not until you are sure of the tool and can control run-out. If you run to a template you'll want a template guide, which fits into the router base and runs against the template and prevents the bit from cutting into the template. Use the ½-inch groove cutter. The ¼-inch groove cutter is good for grooving in drawer bottoms in lieu of a table saw, as well as for curved grooves for tambour doors or chair caning. For grooving you need a fence attached either to the router base for grooves close to an edge or to the work that the router base runs against for grooves farther in. The radius cutters will work the edges and corners of tabletops or rails and pedestal parts, also chair parts. If the part or top is on the small side, you can feed it into the router. Screw a piece of ½-inch plywood to the router base and then secure the plywood to your work-table or bench, allowing the router to fit underneath. Rub the plywood liberally with paraffin. Feed a sample piece into the cutter to be sure the cutter height is adequate to give the full radius before milling your stock. No fence is needed, as the follower is on the cutter. Ball bearing followers are best. Hold the stock firmly to avoid chatter as you mill, but don't press hard on the follower or you'll burn the stock. (Don't stay too long in one place or you'll burn as well.) Watch the grain. If the cutter picks up the grain, back the work into the cutter instead of going forward. You can take several cuts in-stead of one where the grain is kinky to avoid breakout. Always disconnect the power source when changing cutters and wear eye protection when working. Wear goggles if you don't wear glasses. Dovetail and hinge butt templates allow easy joining and mortising for pro-duction work and are available from your dealer. A plastics trimming cutter is also available for trimming laminates in countertop work. A great variety of mold-ing and shaping cutters can be purchased as well. This is a high-utility, portable tool that can be installed in a

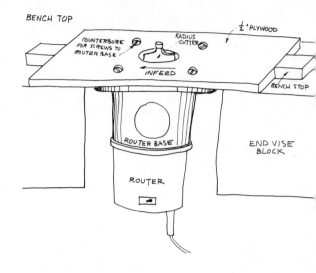

table and used with various templates. The portable router is the best tool for rounding edges and removing stock before carving. I prefer a dado set on a table saw for grooving because it's quicker and easier to set up. A shaper is much better than a router for production milling because it's designed to handle the load. So just as the radial arm saw can do just about anything, according to the literature the manufacturers publish (including cutting your arm off), the router is best for a limited portable operation rather than a wide variety of mortising, grooving and shaping.

• *Sanders.* Belt 3 x 24 inches, 60X, 80X belts, one box of ten each. The abrasive belts and the 3- x 24-inch capacity machine will take care of your rough sanding requirements, a highly laborious operation by hand. Narrow stock such as rails and stretchers can be sanded directly from the thickness planer. On wider work like tabletops the jack plane and smooth plane are best used to remove some of the ridges the thickness planer knives leave across the grain. These ridges are not always apparent but are always there and are accentuated in the finish. The plane shaving, many times thicker than what you remove with a pass of the sander, can actually save time and save on belts. For hardwood start with 60X on a wide surface or 80X on narrow stock. Start with 80X on softwood. Disconnect the power source before installing or removing a belt. Stand the machine on its front pulley and push down until the pulley engages in a retracted position. Or if your machine has a lever on the right side between the pulleys, pull it out to remove the belt. Slide the new belt over the pulleys with the arrow printed on the inside of the belt on top of the pulleys and pointing forward. Push the front pulley in or move the lever back flush against the machine. Turn the machine upside down and adjust the alignment screw on the left side of the front pulley to position the belt track even with the edges of the pulleys. A fractional turn either way will usually make the correction needed. Make sure the belt does not contact the sander frame.

You're now ready to sand. Keep your arm parallel to the grain. You can angle the sander for fast shear cutting, but it is best not to go across the grain too quickly because the scratches are not always entirely removed and can show up in the finish. Keep the sander moving and be sure to cover the entire surface including ends and edges. Keep the sander flat on the work. Avoid tilting; it leaves prominent dents in the work that are hard to get out. The work must be held firmly, either with bench stops or clamps. Keep the sander away from your body and avoid loose clothing that could become engaged in the belt. Keep tools and other blocks of wood away from your work so they don't get fouled in the belt. Keep your machine cleaned out either with a vacuum cleaner or air hose. Use a machine with a vacuum bag attachment, known as a dustless model. While it is not entirely dustless, it's a vast improvement over models without vacuum bags. Empty the bag when it's half full or less to keep the dust pickup operation working at maximum capacity.

The weight of the sander itself is adequate for the job. Applying weight to speed up the operation results in slowing up the job and heating up the machine. It's better to use a fresh belt or a coarser grit. Be sure the cord length will reach over the entire surface and that it

LAP JOINT WITH CEMENT

DIRECTION OF ROTATION
PNEUMATIC SANDER DRUM

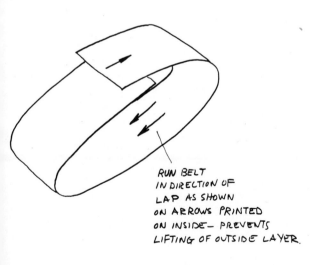

RUN BELT
IN DIRECTION OF
LAP AS SHOWN
ON ARROWS PRINTED
ON INSIDE— PREVENTS
LIFTING OF OUTSIDE LAYER.

will not catch anywhere; this will jerk the sander up short and cause marks on your work. Sometimes I work with the cord over my shoulder to avoid backing the sander onto it. The high frequencies emitted by sanders, especially when used for long periods of time, unquestionably can affect your hearing. Get a headset from your nearest welding supplier. You should hand sand from 100X up to shear off the wood fibers, as the belt only works in one direction. A vibrator machine will give the back-and-forth motion needed as well for production work.

• *A pneumatic drum sander* works well on curved pieces such as chair parts. The machine works best if its stand is bolted to the floor or to a bench for vibration-free work. The abrasive sleeve is held in place on the drum by air pressure. You need enough pressure on the 2-inch drum so you can't feel the steel shaft that passes through the center. The softer the pressure, the rounder the sanding across the piece. You can tell by the feel of the drum once you've got the pressure necessary for the amount of roundness you want. This machine will spew dust. You're best off with a cap and a respirator if you don't have a vacuum system. Being near an open window helps. Check the lap joint on the belt so you sand in the direction of the lap, not against it, which can cause the lap joint to open up. If you find you're sanding against the joint, deflate the drum and reverse the sleeve end for end. I work on the underside of the drum, holding the work up against the sleeve.

The machine is a sander, not a shaper, so it will follow the contours of the piece as it is. Do not expect the machine to iron out bumps. Your curves must be filed continuous before sanding. I find it best to have the coarse grit on the larger diameter drum to minimize lumps and the finer abrasive on the small drum. Keep a firm grip on your stock but do not apply excessive pressure against the drum, especially at the ends of your work, or you'll round off where you wanted a sharp edge. Also, you need to hand sand after this operation because of the one-direction sanding. The pneumatic sander is a great labor saver for rough sanding on curved work, so if you anticipate sanding on curved work, this is a good machine. I own one and use it mostly on chair work after planing in and filing the curves with Surform files and cabinet scrapers. As you work, watch that you don't run off the end of the drum and hit the retaining nut, which will dent your stock. The machine is nearly maintenance-free. There are usually grease fittings on the shaft bearings, which require lubrication. If the drums develop objectionable leaks, send them back to the factory for an airtight seal replacement. Avoid using abrasive sleeves that are worn; this builds up excessive heat that can cause wear on the rubber and canvas on the drum. Also, keep the drum inflation sufficient to avoid excessive wear. If you don't have a compressor, a bicycle pump is adequate to inflate the drums and a tire gauge is a useful pressure check.

• *Sanding block, rubber or cork.* You are better off with a cork or rubber block than a wood one because the softness of the material allows the abrasive to conform to wood better. Sand back and forth with the grain after machine sanding. This will shear off the wood fiber nap that develops after one-direction sanding. Work through grades 100X and 120X for an oil finish and use 150X to

220X for urethane. 400X is needed for a smooth finish on maple or birch.

• *Sawhorses, 48 inches long, 32 inches high, two needed.* Stanley brackets provide a quick way to assemble sawhorses using 2 x 4 stock from the lumberyard. Take the time to join the legs permanently to the horizontal. Lay the legs out on the floor or table so they butt together on top and spread 18 inches apart on the bottom. Cut the angle on the legs to allow a 2 x 4 to fit between the top joint of the legs. Nail the legs to the horizontal with 6d finish nails and use glue. Then brace the legs in both directions with a 1 x 6, using 1½-inch #10 wood screws and glue. This will give you a rugged horse for cutting off stock and sanding large tabletops.

• *Saws. Band, 14-inch with ½-hp. totally enclosed motor.* The size of the saw is determined by the wheel diameter, over which a flexible steel saw band is strained. The vertical steel wheels are fitted with rubber tires and have adjustments for centering the saw on the wheel and giving proper tension, depending on the width of the blade. The upper and lower blade supports need to be in alignment so the blade will run through them freely with no deflection. The ball-bearing blade support wheel should be adjusted to run about $\frac{1}{64}$ inch behind the blade. The blade runs through guide pins that must clear the blade by a few thicknesses of paper and run about halfway on the blade so as not to interfere with the teeth of the saw. A ¼-inch fine-tooth blade is about the handiest small shop size and will cut down to a ¾-inch radius. You can break up a shorter radius by a series of tangential cuts. If you have a long curve to cut, especially a compound curve, make a few preliminary cuts into the curve from the edge of your stock so the pieces will be easily set aside as you cut them away and the saw will not get jammed in a long kerf (the slot that the saw cut makes).

Keep the cut continuous as much as possible for a smooth job, and when possible start across the grain. Sometimes it's best to saw apart several pieces that are marked out on a board before actually sawing to the line. Always stay $1/16$ inch from the line so you have stock to smooth away to finish the curve. Keep the guide ¼ to ½ inch above the work so the blade gets full support and do not jam work to the blade. Watch your hand position, particularly near the end of a cut. The band saw is relatively safe, but it won't tell you to get your fingers out of the way. It will saw all that crosses its path very nicely. You can resaw stock by first sawing up to ½ inch of the center of the board with your table saw, then sawing the ½ inch with the band saw. This is the safest way to resaw stock on typical small shop equipment (as opposed to doing the job entirely on the circular saw). Work carefully and with enough light. Use a sharp blade. Dull blades will wander off a line, so it's economical in the long run to replace it with a new one. At best, the band saw is for curved work, while the circular saw is for straight work. The band saw is the best machine for curved work, better than the scroll saw, which uses a reciprocating motion. The band saw makes a continuous cut, whereas the scroll saw cuts only on the down stroke. If you anticipate any quantity of curved work, the band saw is a must.

Backsaw, 12-inch. This is a very fine-tooth crosscut saw with a stiffener on the top of the blade ensuring a

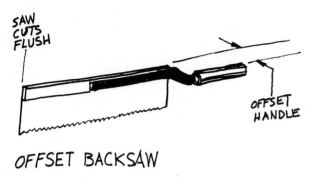

OFFSET BACKSAW

straight true cut. You can clamp a board to your work as a guide to saw against or scribe it with a sharp knife so as to make a positive location for the saw to start. The backsaw will also work fairly well on a short rip cut, especially in softwood for a short tenon (the male member of a mortise and tenon joint) or in cutting dovetail joints, but it is not as good as the ripsaw equivalent, the dovetail or tenon saw. The backsaw can also be used with a wood or metal miter box for accurate miter joints. This is an essential saw for hand-cut joints.

• *Offset backsaw.* The offset handle differentiates this saw from the backsaw. The offset backsaw is used to saw a projecting piece from a glue joint flush to a surface, such as a through tenon. There is no really good substitute tool for this operation, so if you want a neat cut flush with a minimum scratching of the surface this is the tool to own (for a relatively low price).

• *Bench saw,* 10-inch tilting arbor with 1½-hp. totally enclosed motor, combination blade, dado set, planer blade. This is the basic stationary power saw for your shop that does straight-line rip or crosscut cutting. The dado set will cut a rabbet or groove, the planer blade will make a finish cut, and the combination blade will do for both rip and crosscut. The motor is best totally enclosed to keep it dust-free. The tilting arbor is fairly standard today, as opposed to the tilting table. It's easier to tilt the saw than the table. The 10-inch size (meaning a 10-inch diameter blade) can cut stock up to 2½ inches thick fairly well. The miter gauge that runs in the grooves on the top of the table usually has a straight-edge piece of wood screwed onto it that serves as the crosscut fence. Check that the miter adjustment at 90 degrees is in fact a right angle by using your square. The miter stops at 45 and 90 degrees have screw adjustments if any correction is needed. The rip fence should be parallel to the blade so the stock won't bind. Check that the distance is equal from the fence to the grooves in the top of the table at each end, as the blade runs parallel to the grooves.

A saw guard is available to protect the operator's hands from coming into contact with the blade. Wear goggles or your glasses to protect your eyes from flying bits of wood when using the bench saw. Your eyes tell you when your hands are too close to the blade. I personally find the guard annoying, since it prevents me from seeing the blade easily. I feel you are safest when you can see where the danger is rather than have the danger covered. If the distance between the fence and the blade is too narrow for your hand to pass through easily, use a push stick to move the stock by the blade. A push stick is a piece of wood with a notch cut in it that fits over the back edge of your stock and keeps your hands away from the blade. Be sure to push the stock through, beyond contact with the blade, to avoid the blade's catching the stock and whipping it back toward you. The blade turns toward the operator. The combination blade may be kept just high enough to cut the stock because the blade is set to give the teeth clearance. The planer blade is hollow ground and so has to ride higher above the stock so that the narrower, center part of the blade provides clearance and minimizes burning. All blades must be kept sharp and set as required. They must also be kept clean and free of gum, sap, or resin, which causes the blade to bind in the stock.

You can have a splitter guard installation to the rear of the blade, which prevents the stock from squeezing in

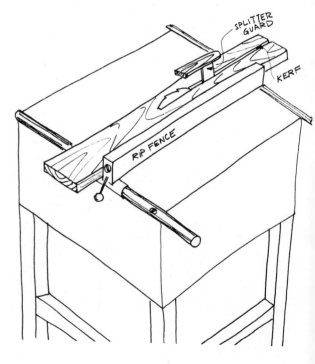

Bench saw with rip fence and splitter guard

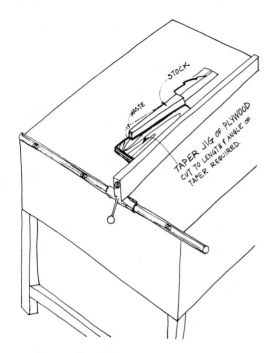

Cutting tapered legs on bench saw

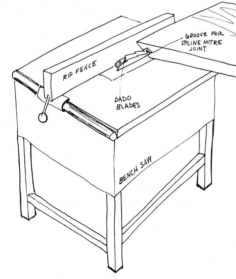

Cutting groove for spline miter joint on
bench saw

on the blade. Or you can make the cut with a lower setting of the blade first feeding in slowly. I don't use a splitter because I find its alignment with the blade is important to be effective and can be time-consuming to maintain. If you have long stock you can go around to the back of the table halfway through the cut to pull the remainder through. Otherwise you need additional support to hold up the stock. Be sure you have enough space when sawing long or wide stock to avoid hitting anything that can cause the job to be stowed. If you do get hung up, hold onto the stock and lower the saw blade all the way down and shut the machine off until you are sure there is enough clearance to finish the cut. Another way to handle the long stock in limited space is to cut halfway and go end for end on the stock, so you finish cutting into the center from the other end. It's safer to lower the blade than to lift the stock up from the blade, as the stock must be lifted vertically so as not to bind.

If the rip fence is used as a stop when crosscutting, a block must be clamped to it that stops short of the blade. The thickness of the stock block provides clearance so the cutoff doesn't jam between the blade and the fence.

The rip fence is used also for taper cuts commonly found on table legs. You need a plywood guide board or jig cut to the length and angle of the taper required. Set the fence from the saw the width of the guide board plus the width of the stock. Feed what will be the top end of your table leg into the saw first. Usually a taper on the inside adjacent surfaces is enough. Often, when all four sides are tapered, the furniture legs seem to kick in or converge at the base.

Stock can be run vertically against the rip fence; this

is commonly done cutting through mortises and tenons. It is important to hold the stock firmly against the fence; paraffin applied to the saw table and fence helps the stock to slide smoothly. The saw table should be kept lightly oiled to keep it free from rust. Spline grooves on mitered edges are also run against the fence with the saw blade at a 45-degree angle. Use the combination blade for thin work or more commonly the dado blades —usually ¼-inch groove a ¼ inch deep for a spline on ¾-inch plywood. This is often done in cabinetmaking.

The dado blades are also used for cutting grooves for sliding doors and for setting in cabinet shelves. Use the miter gauge to steady stock against the rip fence when needed. When cutting blind grooves (unseen on finished work), lower the blade rather than lift the stock up when you get to the end of the cut unless you are an experienced operator. Make a trial run with a scrap piece so you can mark the saw table to indicate where to end the blind groove. The end of the groove can later be squared up with a ¼-inch chisel. The dado blades can also be used to cut the corresponding tongues that fit in the grooves by making an equal cut from each side.

• *Crosscut saw, 12-point.* This is a fine-tooth crosscut finish saw. Unlike the backsaw, it has no stiffener on the top of the blade. This is the saw carpenters use for finish work. You can use it in the shop for cutting plywood and all finish cuts in lieu of the table saw. It's a good saw to have on the job when installing built-ins. Because of its length, it's a relatively fast-cutting saw compared to the backsaw.

• *Cutoff saw, portable, 6¾-inch.* Get a portable saw with a clutch. The better saws allow for slippage if the blade should jam, which prevents the saw from jumping

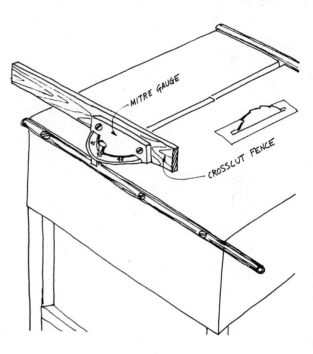

Bench saw with miter gauge and crosscut fence

out from the kerf and into you. Set the saw down on its base but not on the guard. Be sure the guard operates freely and that you have adequate clearance under the saw. Support the work so that the pieces will not bind against the saw blade as the cut is completed. Block up your work so the waste will fall off when the cut is complete. This saw saves a great deal of time in cutoff operations. It's commonly used in construction work for framing up and for cutting plywood. In the shop it is used in lieu of the more expensive radial arm saw. I think the radial arm saw is a far more dangerous tool than this cutoff portable saw. You can get a reasonably straight cut with this saw if you run it against a straight edge that is clamped to your work; a good application for this is a large tabletop where it may be more awkward to bring the work to the saw than the saw to the work.

• *The dovetail saw* is a small backsaw with rip teeth. Dovetailing is a rip cut. On softwood you can get away with a crosscut saw; the chatter is minimal. However, on hardwood you really need a fine-tooth ripsaw for the best work. So if you plan hand-cut dovetails in any quantity you are well advised to own a sharp dovetail saw. You can have your hacksaw filed to create a rip-tooth edge.

• *Ripsaw.* The ripsaw is the correct saw to cut with the grain by hand. It is distinguished from the crosscut by the fact that is has a chisel tooth as opposed to the pointed tooth of the crosscut. The chisel tooth makes a clean cut with the grain. The teeth chisel the wood fibers as the cut is made. In the case of the crosscut, the pointed teeth score the fibers on each side of the kerf and what's left in-between is dust. If you have any

73

amount of ripping to do by hand you should own a sharp ripsaw. The teeth are easily filed at right angles to the face of the saw when the saw is clamped in a file vise or between two boards. The ripsaw is only suitable for rip cuts. If used as a crosscut saw, it will splinter the wood on the underside of the kerf.

• *Radial arm saw.* How would you like to use a bench saw turned upside down and on rollers? I'll grant you the saw can do everything the sales literature claims. But it's basically a cutoff saw for the wood, your arm or whatever crosses its path as it comes forward, with the saw tending to advance itself in the kerf. Maybe I'm a lily, but I don't need the excitement of trying to rip with it or cut dados with it, or miter, or cut tenons. I go for the saw underneath, out of the way where it belongs, with enough cranked up to do the job required. I don't need to see the groove I'm cutting. If you've seen one, you've seen them all, and the fence on the bench saw will maintain the distance you call for. So unless you have a production cutoff situation, give me the bench saw, a far safer and more accurate machine.

• *The sabre saw* is a portable power-reciprocating saw for curved work. In construction it is commonly used to cut out counters for sinks. In the shop it is used for curved work that would be awkward to handle on a band saw. Unless you anticipate this type of work it is not needed initially.

• *The scraper* is used primarily on hardwood to smooth the surface and, unlike the plane, is not significantly affected by change of grain. The scraper makes a finer cut than the plane and should be used after planing on solid wood. If you have a facing glued to the edge of veneer, the scraper is the tool to make the facing flush. The best scraper for veneer work is the double-handled scraper. The scraper is held at a fixed angle in this case; it has a screw adjustment to control the depth of the cut. You can do the same thing with a cabinet scraper, which is merely a piece of tool steel. You set the angle and control the depth of cut by the way you hold it. Use your thumbs to bend the scraper forward slightly in the center. To start, try it at about a 45-degree angle with light pressure. If you're scraping curved work you'll want a curved scraper or a gooseneck. As with all cutting tools, the scraper must be sharp to work properly. To sharpen, file the edge square with the sides using a flat file. Then dress the edge square with a sharpening stone. Complete the sharpening with a burnisher or screwdriver by taking several strokes on the face near the edge to draw the steel out. Then hold the burnisher at about 80 degrees to the face to roll the drawn edge back, forming a miniature hook. It is this hook or burr that does the cutting, and because it is rolled over, the depth of cut is limited. Therefore it does not pick up much when the grain changes or when the grain is multidirectional, such as in mahogany and birds-eye maple. The scraper is also useful in removing old finishes. When the burr is gone, try restoring it with the burnisher first. It may be all that's needed.

• *Screwdrivers.* Screws are excellent wood fasteners. You should own good oval-handled screwdrivers for #6, #8, and #10 wood screws. The oval handle is desirable because it doesn't slip as much in your hand as a round handle does when driving the screws. Screwdriver bits for your brace are also good. The brace, of course, makes driving the screws much easier. Screw drills that bore the proper diameters for specific wood screw sizes, including countersink or counterbore, also make it easy to drive in wood screws. Putting paraffin or soap in the screws also helps. Use your screwdrivers for screws only—avoid prying with them.

• *Shaper, single- or double-spindle.* The shaper is for production milling of curved pieces, particularly chair legs and rails, moldings and builder's finish stock. On curved work, the pieces are first rough cut 1/16 inch outside the marked pattern, then held in a template or jig. The jig runs along the shaper collar and exposes the stock to the cutter knives, which mill the stock to match the jig. If you get a double-spindle shaper the knives will run clockwise on one spindle, counterclockwise on the other, and you can better cope with change of grain. If you have just the single spindle you must work very carefully if you feed into the grain and may possibly have to climb mill which means moving your stock backward or dragging it over the cutter to keep it from breaking out where the grain changes. Straight shaping is done along a fence, whereas curved work is done from a collar that is about 1/16 inch undersize from the cutters. The best collars are ball or needle bearing rather than a solid steel, which turns with the spindle and can burn you jig. The bearings take up the shaper rpm and allow the collar just to roll with the jig. The best cutters are individually removable for sharpening, unlike the integral cutters. Initial contact with the collar is made from pivoting on a steel pin inserted into the shaper table for this purpose. Wear eye protection here. This is

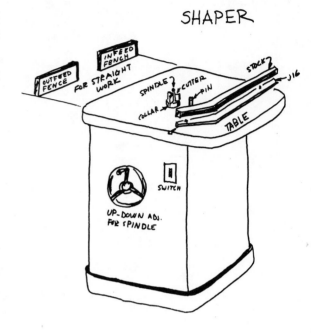

SHAPER

a tough skill to learn from a book, and may be the most potentially dangerous machine in the business. If you're not into production work, steer clear of this one and pocket the change. You can do a reasonable amount of shaping with hand planes, the router, Surforms, then scrapers. The pneumatic drum sander does a nice clean-up job.

• *Shoes.* There seems to be no end to the variety of shoes today. There's a pair for every personality and there's also a kind for work. They're made of leather and your toes don't show through. A crepe or neoprene sole and heel are good. Good workshoes will provide protection for your feet if you drop any tools or stock or step on anything sharp.

• *Shovel, scoop type, or large dustpan.* You need to be able to clean up a shop each day, mainly for fire protection.

• *Spokeshave,* flat malleable iron. The spokeshave literally was once used as the hand tool for fashioning spokes by wheelwrights. It is still useful for shaving spokes or curved chair parts. The tool leaves an unmistakable series of flat surfaces that gives a handmade appearance. The malleable iron resists breakage should the tool be dropped. The best spokeshaves have a screw adjustment for the iron.

• *Squares,* aluminum framing. The framing square is chiefly used in construction to lay out rafters. Because of its size it's also useful in the shop to mark an accurate right angle over the width of a cabinet. The framing square serves as a check against the miter gauge of the table saw. Aluminum is better than steel for this tool:

it doesn't rust and is much lighter. The framing square is also useful in laying out stair stringers. The combination try and miter square is useful on smaller work, though it's not as accurate as the framing square. The rule can slide in the stock of the combination square, so when the stock is held firmly against the edge or end of a board the end of the rule can be a gauge for distance. Be sure the knurled adjustment nut on the stock is tight when the rule is set in position. You can use either a pencil or the scriber found in the bottom of the stock to make your line.

But before you go too much farther you should check to see if your square is square. It's just luck if you get an inexpensive square that's square. Hold the stock firmly against a straight board with the rule extended and secured tight. Draw a line along the rule with a sharp pencil held at about a 45-degree angle and rotate the pencil as you draw. Now flip the stock 180 degrees and see if the rule aligns to the line you just drew. If you are less than $1/32$ inch off in 12 inches it's not too serious. You can correct misalignment by filing down the groove in the stock with a bit file on the high side or you can take the tool back and get a better one. In cabinet work squareness becomes important when fitting drawers and doors. The miter location is useful for laying out miter joints. Some combination squares are equipped with a spirit level which is not very useful as it is only accurate over the length of the stock. Nonetheless it makes the square look a little fancier.

• *Stone*, bench combination coarse and fine India. No tool is much good when it is dull. You need a stone to finish up the sharpening operation. Cutting tools includ-

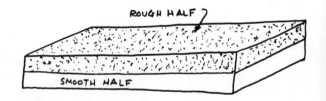

ROUGH HALF

SMOOTH HALF

SHARPENING STONE

ing chisels and plane irons are first hollow ground on a grinder. The angle of the bevel is about 25 degrees and is maintained by the tool holder on the grinder. The curve of the grinding wheel makes the bevel of the tool concave. So when the bevel is set on a flat surface, the front edge and the back edge make contact and the center is high. At this stage, apply a liberal amount of stone oil or kerosene and motor oil mixed 50-50 to the coarse side of your India stone. Keeping the bevel flat on the stone, make half a dozen or so oval strokes. Use the whole stone. You should then have a burr or a roughness on the front edge. Then flip the stone over and apply more oil to the fine side. Again sharpen on the bevel. Then lay the back of the tool flat on the stone and hold it down with your thumb. Take half a dozen or so strokes along the stone until the burr is removed from the back. The burr will now be on the bevel. You must then hone first the bevel and then the back alternately using lighter pressure and fewer strokes until the burr is removed altogether. This is somewhat like breaking a piece of wire by bending it back and forth. If you've done the sharpening accurately and have maintained the bevel angle and held the back of the tool flat on the stone, your chisel or plane iron should now be razor sharp. The oil is used as a lubricant and prevents the stone from being clogged by particles floating off the steel. The best-quality stones are oil impregnated, so you can add oil when you use the stone and it will be adequate. It's best to store the stone in a wooden box and wipe the oil off when through and then soak and dispose of the oily rag in a covered container. There are finer natural stones to put a keener edge on than the man-made India. Washita, soft and hard Arkansas are considerably more expensive but will put a surgical edge on your chisels and plane irons. If you own the best-quality Sheffield steel chisels you'll want one of these better stones, and the tool will be correspondingly sharper for a longer period of time. You should keep the edge of the tools square with the sides. You may want to round the corners of the plane iron to prevent digging in. An alternative to oil stones that I use is a Belgian stone. I prefer using water to oil as a lubricant because it eliminates cleanup. However these stones are hard to come by and oil stones are readily available. So you will probably end up with an oil stone. You can sometimes find whetstones at antique auctions.

• *Tape, 12-foot steel measuring.* Most tapes have a clip to attach to your belt. A ½- or ¾-inch tape is wide enough. Get one with a stop that holds the tape in a fixed position. The 12-foot length is adequate for most of your layout requirements. Never buy a tape less than 8 feet long because you will run out when measuring a standard 8-foot-long sheet of plywood. The tape is handier and more compact than the traditional folding rule. The folding rule, however, is still useful for interior diagonal measurements to check a cabinet for squareness when gluing up.

• *Trash barrel* with cover, metal. It is absolutely essential to store waste in a shop. It must be covered and set aside as a fire prevention measure. A small shop can easily use at least two 20-gallon barrels.

Projects

By now you've learned something about tools and what they do. Now you will learn something about woods and projects that you can make. The intent here is to develop your own ideas from concept to reality rather than meticulously following The Plan. Yes, there is merit in a well-executed reproduction, but remember that today's originals can be tomorrow's antiques. At any rate, bear in mind that what you make is a function of wood, tools and imagination. And everyone makes mistakes. One of the biggest differences between the amateur and the professional is how well the mistakes are covered and how well the wedges, shims, and gluing are done.

Some time ago, as an employee of a Scottish contractor in New England, I found myself up in the air two stories on the plate, which is the horizontal framing member the rafters are toenailed into. We were doing an addition on a colonial-style home. I'd previously cut the rafters, marked off from a tested pattern, to fill in on one side of the ridge board. Apparently, thinking back, the ridge board may have been warped some, or maybe it was the plate. At any rate, I heard down on the ground from the boss, "Son, that rafter is short on one end." Well, I'll be damned if I didn't lift it out of place and attempt to examine it up there on the plate to find where the short end was. So if you find it short on one end sometime, put in your wedge or shim and make it work; do it as well as you can, and be a pro.

Shelves

Shelves are probably the most common woodworking requirement in the home or apartment. Invariably there are more things to put away and get off the floor than there is space available. A shelf is the simplest of all storage solutions. It is basically a surface supported from the wall at various heights and in various widths. When you have a number of such surfaces it is often convenient to enclose them in a cabinet. However, there are times when a single shelf or two of the proper size is all that is needed. And there are times when a shelf can be a relatively inexpensive yet entirely satisfactory and good-looking solution because, unlike a cabinet, it does not hog wall space. For example, take a plank sideboard shelf in a dining room for use as a buffet with a drawer under it for tableware in lieu of the more expensive sideboard. A typical place setting is accommodated in a 14-inch square, so if you wanted a buffet for six you'd have a plank 14 inches wide and 84 inches long. For rigidity it should be 1½ inches thick. You may want to make the sideboard a wall-to-wall installation in

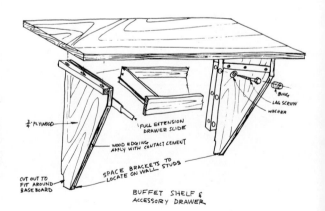

BUFFET SHELF & ACCESSORY DRAWER

your dining room rather than use a bracket support at each end.

I use light Philippine mahogany (tan) with a marine finish for this project. If you want a deeper color use the dark Philippine mahogany or stain the light a shade deeper. Mahogany is often used in boat work because it's stable and looks well with a urethane finish. You can buy it in the rough, 8/4 thick (thicknesses of hardwood lumber are noted by the quarter inch). You can then have the stock milled to 1½ inches and dressed on four sides. The chances are you will have two boards that you will need to glue up. If the boards are somewhat warped, the ½-inch milling tolerance will usually take care of it. However, if you live in an area where milling facilities are not readily available and you want to dress the stock on your own, you'll need a jointer plane and it will take a fair amount of labor. Mahogany isn't all that hard, though; I've done it more than once on wide boards.

If you're working by hand it's best to have 6/4 stock instead of 8/4 so you can just skim the surface, but the board must be relatively straight to begin with. Clamp the plank down on a sturdy table and work an area of half the length at a time. Plane across the stock on about a 45-degree angle. This will give a shear cut, which is desirable on multidirectional grain like mahogany. Use a straight edge to check for flatness as you work. Also check for flatness along the length. The best way to work with the grain is using a two-handled scraper, which will clean up the plane marks. Theoretically both sides of the plank should be surfaced parallel, which is done automatically with a machine. However, it is not absolutely essential so long as the top side is flat. The best clamps for holding boards down to a table are hand screws. I use the 14-inch length jaw. Actually, there is only about a 7-inch clamping surface, but because of the twin screws in each clamp the clamping pressure can be quite effective. Open the clamp to the desired width with the jaws parallel, then slightly close down on the outside screw. Take the inside screw and close down the clamp, then open up on the outside screw. This method will exert pressure on the work all along the length of the jaw. To remove the clamp close down gently on the outside screw. The alternatives to hand screws are bench stops, which are available as standard equipment on better-quality imported workbenches. But where the plank could easily be longer than the workbench, hand screws may well turn out to be the best way to hold the work to the table.

After you have thoroughly scraped the plank, having planed it on all four sides, you will want to sand it to prepare for finishing. The belt sander is the best means of rough sanding for the small shop. Start with 80X. You can then hand sand 100X, 120X, 150X, and 220X. If you are hand sanding you'd best start with 60X. Small shop abrasive work is relatively time-consuming compared to the industrial mill work counterpart. If the mill where the stock is planed has a thickness drum sander, one pass through this machine will have the stock abraded to 80X. You could do the job yourself with a belt sander but it is a time-consumer. Clean the plank thoroughly before applying the urethane. As with all natural-finished built-ins, it is desirable to do the finishing in the shop rather than on the job, because in the shop you should be able to have better dust-free finishing conditions. If you finish in the same area that you work in, be sure the dust has settled before you apply the finish. Be sure to have at least one window open for ventilation, as urethane is fairly toxic. Be sure the final coat of urethane is dry at least a day before installation.

To install the sideboard, lightly mark the location on the selected wall. The height should be the same as your dining room table, or 29 inches. The best way to get the horizontal line is to measure up 29 inches in several locations and then to draw to these locations using a 2-foot level, checking that the bubble in the level is centered between the two scribe lines on the vial. Then locate the studs or the structural vertical interior wall supports. They are usually 16 or 24 inches on center from one corner. Try a 6d finish nail about an inch below the line on the wall to locate the 16- or 24-inch spaced studs. Leave the nails in when you've located it. You will know you've located one when the nail has to be driven more than halfway in. If there is no stud behind the nail the nail will run free after an inch or so. You need a cleat or bracket to rest the shelf on that will attach to the studs. This can be a 1½-inch-square section of leftover mahogany; some of this same stock can be used for a brace or leg to support the front of the plank. Screw the cleat to the studs 1½ inches below the top line. Use 5/16-by-3-inch-long lag screws. The best way to lay it out is to mark off the locations for the screws from the nails in the wall. Then the nails may be removed. The lag screws should be used with washers and counterbored 3/8 inch deep if you want to partially conceal the head of the lag screw. The plank is most easily screwed to the cleat from the top with 2½-inch

#10 flat head wood screws, counterbored ½ inch deep. You can then make bungs with a 1-inch plug cutter to fill these holes. The grain of the bung should run with the grain of the plank.

The same procedure can be used to screw the 1½-inch-square leg to the front of the plank; glue should also be used where the leg comes to the underside. The bottom of the leg can then be toenailed (nailed at an angle) to the floor. It's best to drill pilot holes of a diameter slightly less than the 6d finish nail to get the nail properly started at 45 degrees. Other options for the leg are a bracket that can be attached to a cleat on the wall and a cleat on the underside of the shelf made of either solid plywood or a solid wood end — a continuation of the top surface. I personally prefer a bracket because it delineates the surface as a shelf as opposed to a cabinet and gives it a lighter look.

Often, particularly in old homes, the walls are irregular. If you want a tight fit to the wall and the wall surface is irregular, you will need to scribe its contour on the back surface of the plank. With the plank against the wall at its location, hold a sharp #2 pencil vertically against the wall and run it along the wall with the point down on the plank. This will copy off the contour of the wall. If the pencil is not thick enough you may have to put a block behind it. If you are mounting the cleat to the underside of the plank, keep it about ¹⁄₁₆ inch in from the scribe line so that the screws will press the plank tight to the wall. Be sure the edges and corners of the plank are rounded enough to avoid digging in if you brush against them. I generally allow a ¼-inch radius. You can round off with a block plane if you don't have

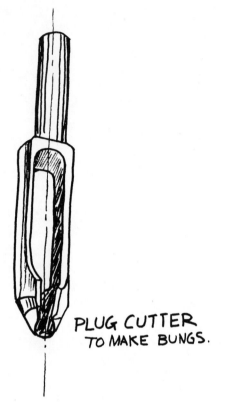

PLUG CUTTER
TO MAKE BUNGS.

too much to do. If you have any large amount, the easiest way is a ¼-inch round carbide cutter in the router. Still another installation method for the sideboard shelf uses a chair rail. However, this will raise the height of the sideboard several inches. The chair rail is a board, often a 1 x 4, whose top edge is about 32 inches above the floor, which prevents chairs from marking the wall. It's an accessory you might want to add if the room doesn't have it. The sideboard can then be mounted flush to the top edge of the chair rail or on top of the chair rail. If you want to paint the chair rail to match the door and window trim, use clear pine, the top grade available in the lumberyard.

Pine is a common choice of wood for shelves because it is available dressed at lumberyards. The standard sizes (in inches) are 1 x 2, 1 x 3, 1 x 4, 1 x 6, 1 x 8, 1 x 10 and 1 x 12. The standard finished sizes are a nominal ¼ inch less in thickness and ½ to ¾ inch less in width. The grades run C select, D select, #1 common, and #2 common. C select is virtually knot-free; D select has small knots; #1 common, called knotty pine, has larger knots; #2 common is high-priced firewood. C select can run more than twice the money than #1 common but is worth it as it is relatively trouble-free. The unit of measure for lumber is the board foot, 12 x 12 x 1 inch thick. Often standard lumberyard sizes are conveniently sold by the linear foot, but the price generally derives from the board foot. Hardwoods in random width and length are usually sold by the board foot.

As an alternative to solid wood, plywood is available in an AB grade. One side of the plywood has an A face veneer and the other a B. There isn't much differ-

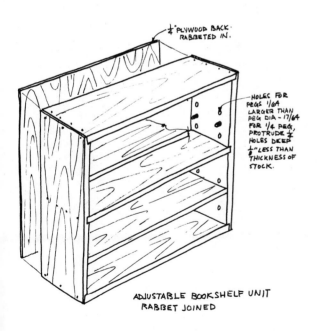

¼" PLYWOOD BACK RABBETED IN.

HOLES FOR PEGS 1/64 LARGER THAN PEG DIA - 17/64 FOR ¼ PEG, PROTRUDE ¼ HOLES DEEP ⅛" LESS THAN THICKNESS OF STOCK.

ADJUSTABLE BOOKSHELF UNIT RABBET JOINED

ence and both are quite good. The B will show very small defects and not quite as good a grain figure. Because plywood is cross-laminated (the layers are glued with the grains at right angles), the material is quite stable. This type of plywood is known as veneer core. Other cores available are lumber, which is solid wood, and particle board, which is compressed wood fibers and glue. Particle board is the most stable core but is extremely hard on all cutting tools except carbide because of its high glue content. Lumber core is the most apt to warp because it is not cross-laminated. My choice if I can get it is veneer core. Plywood is generally sold by the square foot or priced per 4 x 8 sheet. Thicknesses available are ⅛, ¼, ⅜, ½, ⅝, ¾ and 1 inch. Not all of these thicknesses are available in a given veneer. A common commercial shelf material is Baltic birch plywood, an imported cross-laminated birch veneer in 5 x 5 sheets, very strong and quite stable. It is strong because of the high number of laminations due to the thickness of each layer (about ¹⁄₃₂ inch).

Plywood is more convenient than solid wood but must be handled with care, as the veneer thickness ranges from ¹⁄₂₈ to ¹⁄₆₀ inch. Veneer bands are available to conceal the laminated edges and may be applied with contact cement. However, if you prefer a more rounded edge on your shelves, you will need a ¼-inch-thick solid wood band glued on with Titebond. The band should be slightly wider than the thickness of the plywood and flushed off to the surface using the two-handled cabinet scraper. Although a smooth plane can also be used, you run a chance of damaging the veneer because the thickness of the shaving could leave the veneer too thin and you could sand through it when finishing. Often the solid wood band and the plywood veneer don't match exactly even though they are the same wood. This is due in part to the fact that it is not the same log and also because of the way veneer is made. Veneer is peeled from the log much like you peel the skin from an apple. The log is fed into a long knife. As veneer is rolled off the log there is a repetition in the grain figure; the veneer from a log with the same grain pattern is called a flitch. Solid wood, on the other hand, is sawn through the log, so the figure is entirely different and nonrepetitive. Therefore, to match the band to the veneer, it may be necessary to use a little oil stain the same color as the veneer, if possible. As a quicker, less expensive alternate to banding, plywood shelves can be painted to conceal the laminate except in the case of Baltic birch, where the exposed edge is acceptable. Shelf brackets are commonly available in lumberyards and hardware stores. The brackets attach to your studs. Arms of varying widths hook into the brackets to support the shelves. An alternative to brackets is brick or cinderblocks used as spacers between shelves. The shelves can also be nailed or grooved in and nailed in a case or set into a case with adjustable brackets.

The best way to design shelves is to determine the total length needed for the storage requirement and the width, let's say, of the widest book, or whatever. Then consider the wall area and the most pleasing division of the length. In many cases the wall space is so limited that the shape will be dictated. In others a pleasing proportion is often 1 to 2 or 1 to 3, which means the length is two or three times the height. A pleasing height is often eye level.

Tables

A table is basically a free-standing surface with dimensional requirements. It is commonly supported from the floor, although there are those who prefer it suspended from the ceiling. I tend to use the floor because, among other things, the distance the support pieces must cover is less.

One of the simplest and most commonly used designs is the Parsons table. The thickness of the top is generally 1¾ inches and the legs are generally 1¾ inches square. The height is generally 15 inches, the width 18 inches, and the length up to 60 inches. This table would usually be used in front of a chair or sofa as a coffee table. If used by a sofa as a side table the height should be 19 to 20 inches. One of the best choices of wood is red oak because it glues up almost invisibly and the grain pattern is pronounced. If you don't have milling equipment, have the stock dressed on four sides. Then arrange the planks to form a pleasing grain pattern on the top. Mark the arrangement of the planks and apply glue to the edges. Clamp the planks together, checking the alignment, and alternate the bar clamps over and under every 12 to 18 inches. Clean the squeezed-out glue from the planks with a moist rag after clamping up. Check the top for flatness with a straight edge. If it's not quite flat,

Butcher block coffee table, maple, pegged mortise and tenon joints, 18 x 48 x 15 high

an adjustment in the clamping pressure can correct the situation. Apply more clamping pressure to the convex side and slack off a little on the concave. (The best way to be sure the edges fit well is to trial clamp the top without glue.) Let the glue set overnight. After removing the bar clamps, square off the ends of your tabletop. You need to allow an extra inch in length for squaring off.

The legs are best joined to the top with a mortise and tenon joint. The mortise is a rectangular slot about a third the thickness of the stock. From the edge, lay out a mortise ⅝ inch wide and ⅝ inch in from the edge, 1½ inches deep. This is a through mortise and can be chiseled out, sawed out, drilled out or mortised with a hollow chisel attachment on a drill press. Or perhaps you have access to a mortising machine. I use a ⁵⁄₁₆ hollow chisel on a drill press. With the mortises cut, place the legs in position on the underside of the table. Mark off the mortise location on the legs and cut the tenons either with a hand saw or a table saw. The tenon must be cut accurately to fit into the mortise. You should be able to partially assemble the joint by hand, but it should not be a sloppy fit. The glue is effective only when there is a slightly tight fit. For neatness, the width of the tenon is slightly less than the width of the stock, so ¼ inch of the tenon can be removed on the inside. The tenon can only go in so far. It is stopped on the sides by the shoulder and on the edges by the haunch. The joints should be clamped together and the glue allowed to dry for several hours. For further strength the joint may be pegged together using a ½-inch dowel which fits into a ½-inch hole drilled 2½ inches deep. The peg should be glued in and wedged. To wedge the dowel,

Through pegged mortise and tenon joint, detail

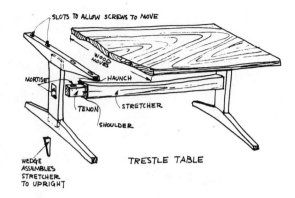

SLOTS TO ALLOW SCREWS TO MOVE

WOOD MOVES

MORTISE

HAUNCH

TENON

STRETCHER

SHOULDER

WEDGE ASSEMBLES STRETCHER TO UPRIGHT

TRESTLE TABLE

make a cut through the center about two-thirds the length and put the dowel in the hole with glue. Then drive a wedge into the saw kerf and use glue.

The mortise and tenon joint is one of the strongest joints in woodworking. Its strength derives from gluing long grain to long grain and joining single pieces with no internal parts to become loose. Historically, the joint was used in framing up buildings in the days when labor was exchanged and time was not so critical. The joints were often pegged together rather than glued. If glue was used it often deteriorated, so the peg became the means of holding the joint together. The mortise had a disadvantage in that it weakened the timber somewhat and invited rotting and termites when used in the sills, the horizontal members that rest on the foundation. One of the best uses for mortise and tenon joints in furniture is in chairs where there is maximum stress on relatively light members.

Once the table is together it may be sanded up and finished. The legs can be flushed up to the edges and ends and all edges and corners should be beveled or slightly rounded. Because the legs on a Parsons table are relatively short, it is not necessary to taper them for lightness. If you do, taper the inside edges only. There are alternatives to the four-leg system. A trestle can be used set in 6 inches or so from the ends. The trestle can either be made straight or sculptured or the entire base can be made laminated and sculptured.

A dining table can be considered an enlarged coffee table. Whereas the design requirements of a coffee table call for the length of the table to be about three feet less than the length of the sofa, the design requirements of a dining table are based on the number of people to be seated. Allow approximately a 16 x 24-inch space per person. The normal height today is 29 inches. When building a dining table select the best planks for the top, then build the base or pedestal with the remainder. I find the trestle is the most satisfactory support on a dining table because it creates the least interference with your knees. The best way to design the trestle is to draw a side and end view full size on wrapping paper which you can tape to a flat wall to work from. Philippine mahogany with a marine finish makes a nice dining table. After you have cut out and assembled the trestle you can glue up the top. After removing the clamps it's best to take a

Dining table, white pine, 48" diameter, 29" high. Made entirely with hand tools

Dining table and benches, walnut
Table, 36 x 72 x 29. Benches, 18 x 72 x 17

Continuous leg coffee table, 20 x 45 x 18

plane and remove the high spots before starting in with a belt sander. I generally hand sand after using 80X abrasive on the sander. As on the coffee table the top

Solid walnut oval dining table, 44 x 70 x 29, first view

second view

must be squared up and the edges broken. I fasten the top to the trestle with lag screws. The slots in the trestle need to be slotted so the screw can slide back and forth as the top expands and contracts from moisture.

Dining set, high chair and chest, cherry

Chairs

Chairs require good joints to last, and are the most difficult piece of furniture to make. The standard dining seat height is 17 inches. The chair is best drawn full-size front and side views. Chairs are generally more shaped than table pedestals. The easiest way to keep the shape uniform is to cut the curve into the side frames after they are glued up. The first frame is marked off from the drawing; it can become the template for the remaining frames. The most expedient way to cut the curve is with a band saw. Stay $\frac{1}{16}$ inch outside the line. The work can then be filed and abraded to the line. A pneumatic drum sander is a great help on curved work, as is a router with $\frac{1}{4}$-, $\frac{3}{8}$- and $\frac{1}{2}$-inch radius cutters. I generally use slats recessed into grooves in the chair seats and backs. The slats are glued and pegged into place. The seat slats are generally $\frac{1}{2}$ inch square and the back slats are generally $\frac{1}{2}$ inch wide and $\frac{5}{16}$ inch thick. The angle of the seat to the back is about 110 degrees, the angle of the seat to the horizontal, about 7 degrees. The depth of the seat is about 16 inches, the width 18 to 20 inches. Rocking chairs are generally 15 inches high and require a pilot model to check the balance.

If you are making any quantity of chairs or want to develop a good chair of your own, a pilot model is absolutely essential (in addition to the drawing). You may want to arrange to visit a chair factory. There are many solutions to chairs besides the traditional that range from stump carvings to stuffed laundry bags and include laminating and carving techniques. Production techniques include jigs, steam bending and vacuum

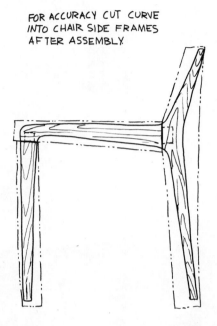

FOR ACCURACY CUT CURVE INTO CHAIR SIDE FRAMES AFTER ASSEMBLY.

Conference chair, cherry, flexible slatted seat and back, 24 x 24 x 32

Slat rocking chair, oak, 32 x 22 x 32

Slab rocking chair, oak, 33 x 23 x 33

Rocker with adjustable head-
rest and back angle, cherry,
slatted seat and back,
26 x 32 x 34

Rocking bench, oak,
23 x 56 x 33

Oak bench, 23 x 84 x 36

Swivel rocking chair, walnut, 32 x 22 x 34, side view

front view

forming. Again a model is needed. Living room lounge chairs are usually an inch or so lower than dining chairs and 6 inches or so deeper. Often 6-inch pincushion latex rubber or polyurethane foam is used for seat and back cushions. The seat cushion can be supported with slats or plywood and the back cushion by slats or spindles. There is a wide variety of good-quality upholstery fabrics to choose from, including leather and various combinations of synthetics. It is best to make chairs in sets of six or more, because of the specialized operations. Almost any one of the hardwoods is a good choice for chairs. I personally prefer cherry, walnut, or white oak.

Beds

A bed is basically a support for a mattress. You don't really need a box spring. Many doctors feel that ¾-inch plywood under a 6-inch latex rubber mattress is the best support for your back. The plywood can be supported by a frame underneath or be held up by four legs and rails and the traditional headboard and footboard. I personally prefer the headboard and footboard because it's more comfortable to put pillows against the headboard than the wall. The headboard is similar to the back of the sofa. If you make the bed 30 inches wide with one high side you have a sofa. Because beds and sofas are bulky, they are best made in a knockdown design. You can use standard bedrail hardware or screws. I generally use a mortise and tenon with a knockout wedge. The wedge goes straight through the post and can be knocked out from the inside and disassembled. The headboard and footboard can be slatted and the slats can be shaped or they can be plywood (either painted or veneer) and the rails can be grooved to fit over the ends. There is room under the bed for storage for either another bed with folding legs, a trundle, or a drawer to put linen in. The drawer can be spline-mitered or dovetailed together.

Dovetailing is the strongest joint in woodworking. It is similar to the mortise and tenon except for the wedge-shaped members. The joint can be quickly cut on the router with a dovetail template. If cut by hand the pins are generally a third the size of the tails. And the angle of the pins is about three to one — 3-inch rise, 1-inch run. Lay out the dovetail starting with a half pin on each edge. Then space the other pins at a 3 to 1 ratio, the space being three times the area of the pins. Cut the pins square to the end of the board and chisel out in between

Knockdown mortise and tenon joint for bed or sofa rail, held together firmly by wedge driven through slot

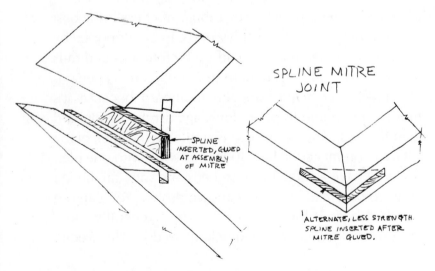

SPLINE MITRE JOINT

SPLINE INSERTED, GLUED AT ASSEMBLY OF MITRE

ALTERNATE, LESS STRENGTH. SPLINE INSERTED AFTER MITRE GLUED.

the pins, cutting halfway from each side with a slight undercut toward the center. Work with the bevel of the

Bed with headboard and drawers, white oak, 39 x 78 x 16, headboard 36 inches high. Drawer side mortised into drawer front. Half-blind handcut drawer side to drawer front dovetail. Alternate with groove for drawer side shown upper right.

chisel toward you or down.   A through dovetail is exposed from both sides. A half-blind dovetail is used at the junction of the drawer front and side and is visible only from the side. Once the pins are cut and the waste chiseled out, the pins become the template to mark off the tails. Hold the pins firmly to the inside face of the board and flush to the end. Then trace off the pins. The depth of the pins and the tails is scribed off with a marking gauge, the gauge distance being determined by the thickness of the stock or, in the case of drawers, the thickness of the drawer sides. The drawer front is usually ¼ inch thicker than the drawer sides. The success of the dovetail joint depends on accurate sawing that splits a sharp pencil line. Work particularly accurately when sawing the tails. Be sure the saw kerf is on the waste side of the line. Chisel out the area occupied by the pins except for the two half pins, which may be sawed out from each edge of the board. The best way to get a clean cut when chiseling to the scribe line is to make a cut about $\frac{1}{16}$ inch in front of it first. Then place the chisel firmly in the scribe line and strike it with a hammer or mallet. It's best to use a mallet with wood handle chisels to save on the handles. The cut in front of the scribe line allows the wood to compress between the two cuts, thus preventing the chisel from cutting behind the line. It is only necessary to make the preliminary cut when first starting. Afterward, when undercutting, the chisel may be put directly back to the scribe line. The undercut only needs to be about 10 degrees. The purpose is to make the center concave so the joint will fit tight on the face. I prefer working on the inside face first when chiseling out dovetails. That way if the chisel is mistakenly driven all the way through it would show only on the inside. The drawer bottom may be glued and nailed or screwed directly to the lower edges of the drawer. Make sure the drawer is glued up square before attaching the bottom. Apply glue on the long-grained surfaces and clamp the sides to the back and front. The pins, of course, will be on the back and front pieces. Drawer bottoms are also commonly grooved in. The groove is commonly ¼ inch wide, ¼ inch deep and ¼ inch up from the bottom except when more space is desired underneath the drawer for reaching under it to open it. The groove may be cut on all four pieces or the back can set flush to the top of the groove on the drawer sides so the bottom will slide under it. This is the way I make drawers generally. When the drawers are fitting into a case, I allow an ⅛-inch clearance for fit all around — ¹/₁₆ inch on each side. I make the drawer sides an ⅛ inch lower than the front on top and the back ⅛ inch lower than the sides. This virtually prevents drawers from sticking in the summer when wood swells. Some woods like mahogany are more stable and a good choice for drawer sides, whereas others like oak, which expand and contract more, are not as good unless given more allowance for movement.

The best way to secure the plywood bedboard to the bedrails is to screw an inch-square strip the length of the rail, about 78 inches, and place the screws about every foot. Use 1½-inch #10 flat head screws. If the bed is wider than 4 feet you'll need to run the plywood across and use two sheets. You will also need a support rail in the center to eliminate sagging. Allow a little space between the two boards. The support rail should be approximately 1 x 3 and it can rest on a cleat with a notch cut in it to keep the rail upright. The size of the mattress or cushions is the basic design consideration for the bed or sofa. Be sure to get the finished mattress size from your foam rubber dealer and allow at least 1 inch extra on the length and width. The best and most resilient mattress material is pincushion latex rubber. Although it costs more than three times what polyurethane plastic foam does, it is well worth it. The plastic foam quickly can lose its resilience. I suggest tapered cushions for the sofa back, also available from a foam rubber dealer.

Where space is at a premium a trundle can be made that fits under the main bed. The easiest way is to screw good-quality casters to a plywood board and attach legs which will fold under when the bed is being stored. The legs need a hook or other locking device to keep them upright when the bed is in use. The legs should be long enough to make a trundle the same height as the main bed, which is commonly 15 inches. I prefer urethane to linseed oil as a bed finish because it is less toxic when dry. However in some cases, to bring out the grain, I have used linseed oil — but never on juvenile furniture.

Cabinetry

I use the term cabinetry to refer to storage pieces which are larger than a single drawer. Building a cabinet gives you the opportunity to use almost all your woodworking skills. It takes a surprising amount of material, and, of course, quality work takes time. The time is spent in joining and fitting. A cabinet should be designed from the point of view of utility and compactness. Consider the size and quantity of the items you want to store and project your future requirements.

Design the cabinet from the inside out. Once you know the height and width required, add an inch or so for clearance plus the thickness of the outside case and the thickness of the shelves if any. You also need to allow an inch or so for the back to set in. Part of the inch is the scribing allowance for installation on an irregular wall. Allow another two inches in width if you have sliding doors. The standard thickness of a cabinet's pieces is ¾ inch except for the back, which can be as thin as ¼ inch.

If you have sliding doors, the first door is generally set in ¼ inch from the front face of the cabinet and runs in a track ¼ inch wide cut about ⅛ inch deep in the bottom and about ½ inch deep in the top. Tongues are generally cut on the top and bottom of the plywood door about $\frac{1}{32}$ inch less than the width of the groove to guide the door in the track. The clearance between the doors is usually ⅛ inch. The door height is usually about $\frac{3}{16}$ inch less than the door opening plus the depth of the track grooves to provide enough clearance to insert the tongue on the top of the door into its track and still allow the bottom tongue to clear the bottom edge and drop down into its track. There will still be about $\frac{3}{16}$ inch of the tongue on the top of the door left to run in the groove. The edges of the tongue should be rounded slightly; beeswax makes the tongue slide more easily in the groove. You need a recessed pull in a sliding door. The

Wall storage cabinet, African mahogany, 12 x 48 x 24

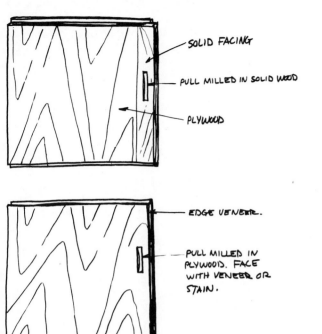

SOLID FACING

PULL MILLED IN SOLID WOOD

PLYWOOD

EDGE VENEER.

PULL MILLED IN PLYWOOD. FACE WITH VENEER OR STAIN.

easiest way to make it is with the dado blades on the table saw. Set the width of cut to ½ inch. Set the fence about ⅜ inch from the blade. Place the door face down, centered over the blade, and crank the dado blades into the door about ⅝ inch deep. Then lower the blade all the way down and remove the door and you will have a recessed pull. It is essential to have the dado blades sharp and to hold the stock firmly. The best way to control the height is to note the location of the adjustment wheel and crank up to it. You need a facing at least 1¼ inches wide of solid wood which is glued to the edge of the plywood to mill the recessed pull into, or veneer or stain the recess. The facing should be cut about ½ inch longer than the desired length of the door and trimmed to length when the door is cut to length. The best tool for making the facing flush is a scraper. Because veneer is so thin, it is desirable in quality work to face the ends as well as the sides of the plywood and then cut miter joints. The width of the facing need only be ¼ inch. It is sometimes easier to glue a ¾-inch facing to two pieces of plywood and to split the facing with a table saw after the glue is dry, leaving two ¼-inch-thick facings on each piece after finishing.

Spline miter joints are the best way to join veneer pieces at the corners. Use the planer blade on your saw. Make sure it's sharp. Run a few scrap pieces to make sure that the 45-degree angle on the saw makes an accurate 90-degree angle when assembled. Check this with your framing square. It is good practice to mark off the miter cut with your framing square and combination square. Make the miter cut on the ends using the cross-cut fence on your table saw. Then make a ¼-inch-wide dado cut at 45 degrees or at right angles to the miter. The groove should be about ¼ inch in from the inside face and ¼ inch deep. Run the stock face up against the rip fence. Run the groove for the spline blind to the front of the case. Either run the dados in from the back, stop short of the front face by ¼ inch, and crank the dados down, or place the face against the fence ¼ inch ahead of the dados and crank the dados up. Then run the cut out through the back. The groove for the back is also run with the dados and should be about ½ inch deep and 1 inch wide; the grooves for the shelves should be ¼ inch wide and ¼ inch deep and stop short of the front of the shelf by ¼ inch. The front of the shelf should stop short of the back of the door by at least ⅛ inch. The splines which fit in the grooves should be about 1/32 inch less than the depth of the grooves and tapered in front to correspond to the runout of the dado groove. Use Weldwood plastic resin powder glue to assemble. If using urethane (which I recommend because it is easier to keep clean), it is best to finish the interior surfaces of the cabinet before assembling. Also, it is easier to clean the glue off a finished than an unfinished surface.

Unlike dovetails, spline miter joints need to be clamped in two directions to ensure alignment. Use softwood blocks to prevent damaging the veneer with the bar clamps. Keep the blocks about ¼ inch from the edges and clean off the glue as soon as possible after gluing up. Be sure to check that the cabinet is square by measuring diagonals. Squareness in cabinets is extremely important for conveniently fitting doors and drawers. The diagonal measurements should be within 1/16 inch of each other. If necessary, clamp across the long diagonal to reduce a discrepancy greater than $\frac{1}{16}$ inch. An alternative to miter joints is rabbet joints. Nail holes can be covered with plastic wood, wood dough, or stick shellac in the appropriate color and screws can be counterbored and plugged with bungs of the same wood as the cabinet. As opposed to spline miter joints, these are quick options for constructing a cabinet. There is nothing wrong with using nails or screws, particularly if the cabinet is going to be painted or stained, thus making the bungs and filler less obvious. An alternative and decorative option for joining a cabinet made in solid wood is through dovetail joints. In this case, the pins are generally on the horizontal members so they show

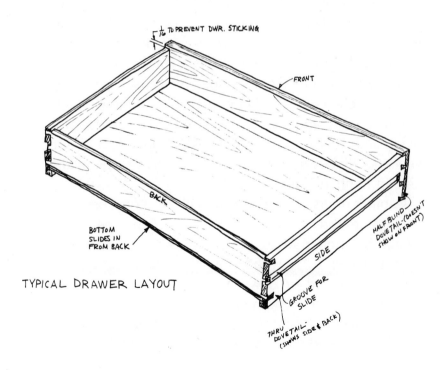

$\frac{1}{16}$ TO PREVENT DWR. STICKING

FRONT

BACK

BOTTOM
SLIDES IN
FROM BACK

SIDE

HALF BLIND-(DOESN'T
SHOW ON FRONT)

GROOVE FOR
SLIDE

THRU DOVETAIL-
(SHOWS SIDE & BACK)

TYPICAL DRAWER LAYOUT

through the sides. This is the strongest as well as the most time-consuming method of hand joining. However, hand-cut dovetails are the mark of a first-rate job. Also, to save on weight and because the dovetail is strong, no back is needed on the case. 1 x 2 cleats glued and screwed to the top and bottom of the cabinet are adequate when used with lag screws for wall mounting.

If you want a project and you've never made a cabinet before, a stationery box for desktop use is a good choice. It can be a box with drawers only or include a small door. It also makes a good gift or a work sample. Another possibility and a fairly useful and simple cabinet is a blanket chest.

Common cabinet veneers include pine, birch, mahogany, walnut, cherry and oak in various grades based on the grain figure. Plywoods are more convenient, more stable, and more easily worked than solid woods. So if you work carefully and don't spoil the veneer, plywood is a good choice. The other possibility—and one which will take more abuse than veneers or plywood—is solid wood and can be any of the woods mentioned above for veneers. Pine is the easiest to buy, being readily available in lumberyards.

Cabinet doors are best made with plywood because it is stable and will not swell up and jam. The edges should be banded to conceal the plywood laminations. An alternative to plywood is a solid wood frame mortise and tenoned or doweled together with slats or a solid wood panel. The mortises should be in the vertical members of the frame and the tenons in the horizontal. If a solid wood panel is inset, a ¼-inch groove

½ inch deep should be cut in the center of the inside edges of the frame. The panel fits all the way into the horizontal grooves and halfway into the vertical grooves of the frame. The grain generally runs vertically, so the wood will be free to expand across the width by going further into the vertical grooves or, if it shrinks, to pull out slightly from the vertical grooves. In addition to sliding, the cabinet doors can be fitted and butt hinges mortised into the door side. The width of the butt hinge should be the thickness of the cabinet door. The mortise is made by carefully chiseling out a slot the depth of the thickness and the length of the hinge. The door commonly fits flush to the front end of the cabinet. Or you can attach a slightly oversized door with a rabbet cut all around the edge. The door stops on the rabbet.

The flush-mounted door is often stopped by a magnetic catch, which consists of a magnet mounted on the inside or shelf of the cabinet near the center and about ¾ inch in from the edge and a metal strike which is screwed to the inside of the door and aligns with the magnet. The magnet has a slotted screw adjustment so the door can be held closed flush to the outside edge. Door handles can be in the form of knobs or carved pulls or they can be inset. For example, you could carve a pull and mortise it into the door, which I do sometimes. There are a number of wood, metal and ceramic commercial knobs available at your furniture, lumber or hardware supply stores.

To lock the cabinet securely I suggest a piano hinge which runs the full length of the door. The piano hinge need not be mortised in as it runs the full length. Piano hinges come in standard lengths and must be cut with a hacksaw to a specific length if the size you need is not readily available. The easiest lock to install is a half-mortise drawer lock. All that is needed is a hole through the door for the barrel of the lock. The hole must be drilled square and located so the tongue of the lock is in from the edge of the door about $1/32$ inch. If you drill the hole by hand, sight the brace or drill to a known vertical such as a window mullion or a door casing. It is best to sight in two directions. Be sure the diameter of the hole is the same as the diameter of the barrel of the lock. Drill through the drawer until the spurr, or center of the bit, protrudes slightly from the underside. Then complete the hole from the other side to avoid splitting out. Mark the location of the tongue of the lock on the inside face of the cabinet and measure in from the face of the cabinet to the face of the tongue. You can then mortise out for the tongue so you can lock the door into the side or divider of the cabinet. You can also lock the door into another door if you put a sliding barrel or flush bolt on one of the doors which allows locking the door from the inside. A full-mortise lock is available as an alternative to the half-mortise lock. A full-mortise lock must be entirely mortised into the side of the door. The keyhole must be located from the front and a key escutcheon mortised into the front face. This is a dressier job than the half-mortise; it is much more work and not necessary unless the inside surface must be free of hardware, such as a writing surface on a desk that folds up to lock the desk front.

Cabinet drawers are more work than doors as fitting includes attaching the sides, the bottom and back. The drawer front is fitted first to go snugly in the opening.

The drawer back is cut the same length if dovetail joints are used and decreased by twice the thickness of metal drawer slides, commonly 1 inch, if they are used. Wood slides can also be used and can be grooved into the drawer sides. Another possibility is a frame which fits under the drawer that it can run on. I tend to use wood drawer slides, which don't rattle so much, unless the drawer must be pulled all the way out without separating from the cabinet, such as a file drawer in a desk. Then metal full-extension slides are needed. The drawer should be at least ½ inch shorter than the depth of the cabinet to ensure that it can close. The drawer sides can be rabbeted and nailed or, for use with metal slides, a sliding dovetail can be cut with a router which allows the side to slide into the front from underneath in a dovetail-shaped slot. Another solution with metal slides is mortising the drawer sides into the drawer front with a series of straight mortises. Drawer handles are similar to door handles. They can either be carved in or knobs can be added. Or in some cases you can reach under the drawer. The drawer front will have adequate clearance once it is sanded in the finishing operation.

The metal drawer slides have slotted screw adjustments for correct drawer alignment. The wooden drawer slides are fitted into grooves in the drawer sides. The drawer is inserted into the cabinet with a dab of glue on the front of the drawer slide so it will stick in position with the drawer closed to the inside of the cabinet. The drawer can be retracted in about an hour. Screw holes in the drawer slide should be slotted if the cabinet is made from solid wood to allow for movement.

Outbuildings

For those of you who want to start a shop but can't clear out your basement, here's a possible solution — an outbuilding. Who knows, you may do such a good job your wife may move out there too. In planning an outbuilding the basic consideration is square footage. Consider the items you need to store on the floor after first getting rid of those you don't need or want. Check the building code in your town to see if a permit is needed for the size you have in mind. Some towns have a minimum size for which a permit is not needed and on which there is no tax assessment. The illustrations shown are for a 7 x 7 building, 6 feet high, with a flat roof. The roof can be a play deck for children with a railing and wire screening. The materials are ½-inch exterior plywood over 2 x 3 studs. The finish is an exterior mahogany stain. The roof is sealed with asphalt cement. Rather than a flat roof you could have a peaked roof with shingles, either wood or paper, as illustrated. You could have a sliding barn door or a hinge door and possibly a hinge window.

The foundation can be poured cement or five standard-size cinderblocks, one at each corner and one in the center. The blocks should be set several inches into the ground. It may be necessary to upend some of the cinderblocks if there is a grade. The floor is supported by a frame of 2 x 4s. Use a straight 2 x 4 and your 24-inch level to check that the cinderblocks are level before laying down the frame, which is a combination of sills and joists. You need enough 2 x 4s for a frame or sills the dimension of the building plus stock for joists, which are

Outbuilding with deck, 7 x 7 x 6

spaced in the frame 16 inches on center. Assemble the frame with 12d common, galvanized nails. If the 2 x 4s are curved or warped, make sure the convex side is up when setting the frame in place to avoid sag. Use three nails in each joist. The hammer commonly used is a 16-ounce one, although those exclusively in the framing trade sometimes use 20-ounce.

Set the frame on the four corner blocks and make sure the center block is located under one of the joists. Check again for level. You may have to place a shim or a thin piece of wood under a low corner. Then drive a 2-foot stake into the ground in each corner flush to the top of the sill and nail the stake to the frame. The stakes can be pointed pieces of 2 x 4s. Galvanized nails are used throughout to minimize rust. To minimize rotting, a wood preservative such as Cuprinol may be applied to the floor joists. It is available in dark brown and may be used as an exterior stain as well. Now nail the plywood floor to the frame. Run the plywood in the direction of the joists so the joint of the 4 x 8 sheet will fall along the fourth joist. Nail the plywood to the joists with 8d common galvanized nails spaced 8 inches apart. Now assemble the four wall frames of 2 x 3s. First frame out the sides of the building, then space the studs 16 inches on center except where allowance is made for a door or a window. The width of the door is generally 3 feet; the window can be standard size or 30 x 30 inches. Deduct the width of the 2 x 3s for the two walls that will fit between the two you have just made. Place the four walls in position on the floor, one at a time, and nail them to the floor flush to the edge with 12d common nails. Now nail the corners together. For added strength it's best to double up on the studs around the door and window and on the top of the wall known as the plate.

Now run 2 x 4 rafters either straight across for a flat roof 16 inches on center or one or two joists 24 inches on center to tie the walls together if a peaked roof is planned. The easiest way to lay out the rafters for a peaked roof is to start with a scale drawing. Then cut two rafters to size and lay them out on the ground to check the angles of the notch or flat that fits on or over the plate and the angle at the ridge. To mark off the rafter angles, use your framing square to measure the rise and run of the angles as scaled from your drawing. The rafters are joined at the ridge by a 1 x 6 board. Nail the board to the rafters on one side, the rafters being 16 inches on center, with 8d common nails and support the ridge in the center of the building at the required height. Then nail down the rafters at the plate. Toenail with the nails at about 45 degrees to attach the rafters to the plate. Toenail the rest of the rafters to the opposite plate and at the ridgeboard. A peaked roof with shingles should not have a pitch less than 4 to 12 — a 4-inch vertical rise to a 12-inch horizontal run. A lower pitch can mean water getting under the shingles.

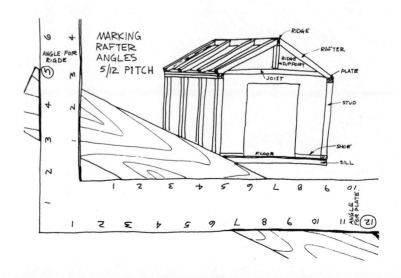

Outbuilding, exterior plywood shown before staining, 7 x 7 x 8½

You can lay the plywood on the flat or peaked roof. Start at the bottom or the edge and work up or across, respectively. To lay a peaked roof, you will need to stand on a staging plank, a 2 x 12, the length of the building, which can be supported by a stepladder on one end and a 2 x 4 arm securely nailed to at least three studs on the other end. Use three nails in each stud and brace the arm with a 1 x 6 board at the end, letting the brace project above the arm to prevent the staging from sliding off. Make sure the arm is horizontal or sloping slightly toward the building, but never away from the building. Try hanging on the arm to check it

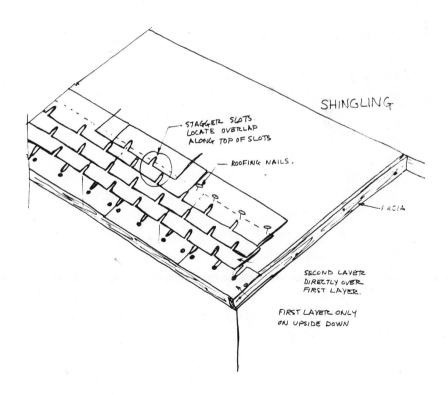

SHINGLING

STAGGER SLOTS. LOCATE OVERLAP ALONG TOP OF SLOTS

ROOFING NAILS.

FACIA

SECOND LAYER DIRECTLY OVER FIRST LAYER.

FIRST LAYER ONLY ON UPSIDE DOWN

for strength before setting the plank on and make sure the stepladder is firmly supported and level. A sturdier staging would be supported on both ends and the ladder resting against the staging. The height of the staging should be about 18 inches below the plate. Nail the ply-wood to the rafters with 8d common nails spaced about 8 inches apart. If you are using paper tab shingles, start at the bottom of the roof and put the first course (row) on with about ¼-inch overhang and with the tabs upside down. Use ¾-inch roofing nails about 1 inch below each slot and at the ends of each shingle. Keep the course straight. If you have trouble keeping the shingles lined up, strike a chalk line to work to. This is a line that is chalked, held taut, then snapped from the middle of the line leaving a chalk line to nail the shingles to. The second course of shingles goes over the first course right side up. Position the nails about 1 inch above the tabs. The third course of shingles goes over the second course down to the top of the tabs. The shingle joints are staggered by cutting the shingle through one tab at each alternate course. One of the easiest ways to cut a shingle is with a straight tinsnips. When you get to the ridge, fold the top of the course over to the other side and nail it down. Then take a series of shingles which have been cut through the tabs and shingle along the ridge, half lapping the shingles over each other. Paper shingling should be done on temperate days. If it is too cold the shingles will be brittle; if too hot, they become easily bruised.

Wood shingles are about four times the cost of paper and take about four times as long to install so unless you are really crazy about wood shingles or intensely dislike paper shingles they may not be worth it. The two last about the same length of time—15 years. Wood shingling is similar to paper shingling. The first course is usually doubled, though both courses are laid with the taper up, and the joints are staggered. Use a 1½-inch shingle nail or clapboard nail. Shingles are often applied with a shingle hatchet, which can both shave the shingles to fit against each other and drive the nails. The best wood shingles are made of clear white cedar which has a natural resin that resists the elements. The shingle courses are commonly spaced 5 inches exposed to the weather. In lieu of the shingle hatchet a hammer and block plane can be used. The shingles do not always require shaving. I often tack a straight edge at the 5-inch mark and butt the shingles against it to keep the courses straight. The ridge of a wood shingle roof is generally two boards called a ridge cap, butted together, running the length of the roof, nailed to each other and to the top course of shingles on either side.

The walls can now be sheathed or covered with the exterior plywood. Butt the plywood up tight to the rafters or roof boards. Space your 8d nails at about 8 inches. Butt the plywood carefully at the corners. Seal with caulking compound. Exterior plywood has a marine glue which, with a preservative stain, makes any further protection unnecessary. However, you may want to shingle the sides or use wood or vinyl clapboards. A portable electric saw is quite useful in cutting the studs, rafters, and plywood, although a hand saw could be used.

The door track is mounted by bolting the brackets to the wall at the roof line. The door can be made from a piece of ½-inch plywood with 2 x 6 braces. The rollers for the track are then bolted to the top of the door and through the 2 x 6 brace at the top. The door can then be inserted in a track and wood stops nailed to the wall at the end of the track. A retainer wheel to keep the door from flapping can be screwed to the wall at the bottom of the door; the wheel adjustment will run along the bottom brace.

The stairs are made from 2 x 6 stock with the treads spaced and grooved in ½ inch deep on a 45-degree angle to the edge every 7 inches. The treads are 24 inches long, as is the height of the rail on the side of the stairs and around the roof. The stairs are toenailed to the side of the building at a 45-degree angle with five 8d

Outbuilding with deck, exterior plywood, mahogany stain, 7 x 7 x 6

common nails on each stringer and supported by a 1 x 4 cleat. At the bottom the stairs are staked to the ground and rest on cement block. The treads are nailed to the stringers with three 12d nails on each end. The top rail supports are toenailed into the roof and caulked with roofing cement. Wire mesh is stapled to the rail and vertical supports around the roof to keep youngsters from slipping through. The rail and supports are 2 x 3 and the stair railing is 1 x 4. Check all edges for splinters after installation. Apply preservative to the stairs and rails as well.

For security, add a hasp and padlock on the door, available at your local hardware store.

The window can slide on a track like the door, as shown. It can be held closed by a hook on the inside which hooks to the wall. You can also buy a standard-size glass window which can be hinged to open out from the side or top or hinged to open in on the bottom.

Considerations

Schools: Pro and Con

On the one hand school is a shortcut to learning woodworking techniques and design. Apprenticeships, when available, can also be shortcuts in learning woodworking. You can't go wrong with some schooling and work experience. However, there is no experience like being on your own in this business or working with a crew. At times it is a pure nightmare. Yet other times, when the work is there and it gets done and installed where necessary and you become known for reliability and quality work, the satisfaction in part offsets the rather meager income. The old adage is true that there is no substitute for experience, particularly experience on your own. You may not learn as much and as quickly as you will at school, but your learning will be from personal conviction and tempered with business consideration, including reliability.

You may want to consider local adult education courses or more formal training, such as Rochester Institute of Technology, School for American Craftsmen, Rochester, New York, or Rhode Island School of Design,

School of Industrial Design, Providence, Rhode Island. You may want to check your library for books on woodworking, including Audel's manuals on building and *The Complete Book of Woodworking* by Charles Heyward. The American Crafts Council in New York City has publications on woodworking. Check your local museum for relevant shows including wood sculpture. Do not ignore furniture stores, where tomorrow's antiques are currently being sold. Remember, antiques are really selected examples of what was once sold new. I don't see much point in paying a premium for something old and rickety or well worn if it could be made new for less and possibly made more sturdy.

As the investment in woodworking can be considerable, I urge you to keep financial records and photographs of your work, whether amateur or professional. Pictures are better than drawings because they show the reality of the work as opposed to the concept. Drawings are useful when they are personally helpful in the execution of the work. If you take your own pictures you will need a good camera, at least two floodlights, and possibly a good seamless paper backdrop. You will also need a tripod. The most compact record is colored slides; you can also make your own album with prints. You can save considerable money over the years with a modest investment in an enlarger and related photographic darkroom equipment for black and white work.

If you do any quantity of work for others you will want to keep financial records by quarters as a basis of comparison and to note your business trends. If you become professional, you will want to know a good accountant and/or be familiar with federal and state taxation as related to the small business, particularly regarding depreciation of equipment, which can be used to offset tax liability on income. You will also want to keep accurate records of materials costs, inventory if any, and bad debts if any. Your state probably has a sales tax for retail sales. You will want a vendor's license, which means you do not pay tax on purchases for resale. You charge a tax on retail sales and usually no tax on wholesale. There is no substitute for retail sales and word-of-mouth advertising. Remember you are working with a material that took years to grow. You should build it, then, for the ages. In the early stages you may find it necessary to build on speculation for a few shows. Have business cards available for distribution. The psychology of your work as an independent is surviving by accepting the challenge of being reliable and doing each job to the best of your ability with the intent and conviction it will be your best work to date.

Design: The Kinds of Things You May Be Thinking About, and Reflections

Design is a bomb, a grotesque. Design is poetry and beauty. It's the reconciliation of the freshness of the moment with experience. It's what you make it, baby. Just don't get too hung up on design and stay loose. Paper and pencil provide the point of reference and shape outside your head. Keep a sketchbook of your ideas and be aware of work that appeals to you, current and antique. Yes, you can draw it, because you have to if you want to make it or do it. Put up or shut up as far as drawing it. As you draw you think — no other way. The concept solidifies some. Sketch several ways, alternate plans. Then comes the framework of dimensions. The inside capacity requirements of a cabinet, the height of a chair, the width of a bed, the number to seat at a dining table, the size of the wall space, the width of the chair, the shape of the dining table as it relates to the floor dimensions, and so on, until all numerical questions are answered. Dark or light wood? Hardwood or softwood? Solid wood or plywood or a combination? Type of finish? Your preference for the given situation and your client's, if made to order — both must be considered. Each requirement can be taken one at a time and answered. So it begins to have commitment as the questions are answered one by one on paper, and the piece begins to evolve.

Your first designs may well be more laborious as each question is gravely considered. In time, though, the answers get easier, a set of responses, your own, evolves for certain combinations of requirements, you begin to piece it together more quickly, philosophy translates more easily to reality, and you enjoy personal growth, or the potential of it. A facility to handle design situations is one of the most satisfying tools and techniques in woodworking and may be the only one money can't buy. And it's never over. Think as you work. That's how subtleties and refinements and evolution happen. And be happy.

Bibliography

Adams, Jeanette, and Stieri, Emanuele. *The Complete Woodworking Handbook*. New York: Arco Publishing Co., 1960.

Anderson, Edwin P. *Electric Motors*. New York: Theodore Audel & Co., 1968.

Brumbaugh, James. *Upholstering*. New York: Theodore Audel & Co., 1972.

DeCristoforo, R. *How to Build Your Own Furniture*. New York: Popular Science–Outdoor Life Books, 1965.

Edlin, Herbert. *What Wood Is That?* New York: Viking Press, 1969.

Feirer, John. *Cabinet Making and Millwork*. New York: Charles Scribner's Sons, 1973.

Gibbia, Salvatore. *Wood Finishing and Refinishing*. New York: Van Nostrand Reinhold Co., 1971.

Grotz, George. *The Furniture Doctor*. Garden City: Doubleday & Co.

Hayward, Charles. *Cabinet Making for Beginners*. New York: Drake Publishers, 1971.

———*Woodwork Joints*. New York: Drake Publishers, 1970.

How-to Associates, ed. *Do-It-Yourself Encyclopedia*. 2 vols. New York: Theodore Audel & Co., 1968.

Irvin, D. *Power Tool Maintenance*. New York: McGraw-Hill Book Co., 1971.

Joyce, Ernest. *The Encyclopedia of Furniture Making*. New York: Drake Publishers, 1971.

Kettell, Russell H. *Pine Furniture of Early New England*. New York: Dover Publications, 1929.

Matthews, John, and Kerr, J. D. *Pictorial Woodwork*. New York: St. Martin's Press, 1971. *Book 1. Background to Wood Construction and Finishes. Book 2. Tools and the Uses. Book 3. Guide to Practical Work.*

Ramsey, Charles G., and Sleeper, Harold R. *Architectural Graphic Standards*. Edited by Harold D. Hauf and Joseph N. Boas. New York: John Wiley & Sons, 1970.

Rockwell International, Pittsburgh. *Getting the Most out of Your Abrasive Tools.*

Getting the Most out of Your Bandsaw and Scroll Saw.

Getting the Most out of Your Drill Press.

Getting the Most out of Your Circular Saw and Jointer.

Getting the Most out of Your Shaper.

Rockwell Router.

Shea, John G. *The American Shakers and Their Furniture.* New York: Van Nostrand Reinhold Co., 1971.

Siegele, H. H. *The Steel Square.* New York: Drake Publishers, 1970.

Sloane, Eric. Museum of Early American Tools. New York: Ballantine Books, 1973.

Trussell, John R. *Introducing Furniture Making.* New York: Drake Publishers, 1970.

Ulrey, Harry F., and Emery, T. J. *Carpenter and Builder's Library.* 4 vols. New York: Theodore Audel & Co., 1970.

Wagner, Willis H. *Modern Carpentry.* South Holland, Ill.: Goodheart-Wilcox Co., 1973.

Willcox, Donald. *Wood Design.* New York: Watson-Guptill Publications, 1968.